Everyman's Poetry

Everyman, I will go with thee,
and be thy guide

Percy Bysshe Shelley

Selected and edited by TIMOTHY WEBB

University of Bristol

This edition first published by Everyman Paperbacks in 1998
Introduction and other critical apparatus
© J. M. Dent 1998

J. M. Dent
Orion Publishing Group
Orion House
5 Upper St Martin's Lane
London WC2H 9EA

Typeset by Deltatype Ltd, Birkenhead, Merseyside
Printed in Great Britain by
The Guernsey Press Co. Ltd, Guernsey, C.I.

British Library Cataloguing-in-Publication Data
is available upon request

ISBN 0 460 87944 8

Contents

ı

Note on the Author and Editor   v
Chronology of Shelley's Life and Times   vi–xi
Introduction   xii

Hymn to Intellectual Beauty   3
Mont Blanc   5
Ozymandias   9
Stanzas Written in Dejection – December 1818,
    near Naples   10
from Julian and Maddalo: A Conversation   11
from Prometheus Unbound   24
The Mask of Anarchy   27
Ode to the West Wind   39
from Peter Bell the Third   42
England in 1819   49
The Cloud   50
Men of England: A Song   52
To a Sky-lark   53
from Letter to Maria Gisborne   56
from The Witch of Atlas   60
To the Moon   64
from Epipsychidion   65
Adonais   68
The Aziola   83
from Hellas (The world's great age begins anew)   84
O World, O Life, O Time   85
One Word Is Too Often Profaned   86
To Jane (The keen stars were twinkling)   86
Lines Written in the Bay of Lerici   87
from The Triumph of Life   89

Notes   98

Note on the Author and Editor

PERCY BYSSHE SHELLEY (born in 1792 at Horsham, Sussex) was eldest son and heir to a landowning Whig MP. At Eton he wrote two Gothic novels. His brief career at University College, Oxford was abruptly terminated in 1811 when he was expelled for refusing to answer questions concerning *The Necessity of Atheism*. In the same year he eloped with and married the 16-year-old Harriet Westbrook by whom he had two children. In 1814 he eloped with Mary Godwin, daughter of the pioneering feminist Mary Wollstonecraft, and the anarchist philosopher and novelist, William Godwin. In 1816 they spent the summer close to Byron at the Lake of Geneva where Mary began *Frankenstein* (published in 1818). In December 1816 Mary and Percy eventually married after the suicide of Harriet. In March 1818 they departed for Italy. During the next four years they lived variously in Bagni di Lucca, Este, Naples, Rome, Leghorn, Florence (where their only surviving child Percy Florence was born in 1819), Pisa and San Terenzo in the Bay of Lerici during the final summer of 1822 where Percy was drowned in a storm on 8 July. At his death Percy Shelley left a large body of unpublished materials including the *Defence of Poetry*, a central exposition of Romantic poetical theory. The range of his achievement and of his writing has not always received due recognition: it included political and philosophical essays and pamphlets, translations, the didactic vision-poem *Queen Mab*, a play (*The Cenci*), poems and lyrical dramas of epic scope such as *The Revolt of Islam* and *Prometheus Unbound*, and a wide range of poems of middle length as well as the odes and lyrics by which he is best known.

TIMOTHY WEBB is Professor and Head of the Department of English at the University of Bristol. His books include *The Violet in the Crucible: Shelley and Translation* (1976), *Shelley: A Voice Not Understood* (1977), *English Romantic Hellenism* (1982), *Shelley's 'Devils' Notebook* (with P. M. S. Dawson, 1993) and *The Faust Draft Notebook* (with Nora Crook, 1997). He has edited a comprehensive edition of Shelley's *Poems and Prose* for Everyman (1995).

Chronology of Shelley's Life

Year	Age	Life
1792		Born 4 Aug. at Field Place, Horsham, Sussex; eldest child of Timothy Shelley, landowning Whig MP, later a Baronet
1802	10	At Syon House Academy, Isleworth, near London
1804	12	At Eton where he is bullied, develops scientific interests and writes two Gothic novels
1810	18	University College, Oxford (Oct.)
1811	19	Meets 16-year-old Harriet Westbrook (Jan.). Expelled from his college with his friend Thomas Jefferson Hogg for refusing to answer questions concerning their pamphlet *The Necessity of Atheism* (published Feb.). Elopes with Harriet and marries her in Edinburgh (29 Aug.)
1812	20	Working on lost novel *Hubert Cauvin*. Visits Dublin; speaks, writes and distributes pamphlets on behalf of Catholic emancipation and Repeal of the Union (Feb.–Mar.). Becomes a vegetarian (Mar.). Lives in Wales, then Lynmouth, Devon, where he is watched by government spies. Moves to Tremadoc (North Wales) in September. Meets Thomas Love Peacock and William Godwin. Writing *Queen Mab*
1813	21	*Queen Mab* privately issued (May). Daughter Ianthe born to Harriet (23 June)
1814	22	*A Refutation of Deism* printed. Elopes with Mary Godwin (27 July); together with Claire Clairmont they tour Continent. Son Charles born to Harriet (30 Nov.)

Chronology of his Times

Year	Artistic Events	Historical Events
1792	Wollstonecraft, *Vindication of the Rights of Woman*	Absent Thomas Paine tried for publishing *The Rights of Man*
1793	Godwin, *Political Justice*	Executions of Louis XVI and Marie Antoinette
1798	Wordsworth and Coleridge, *Lyrical Ballads*	Irish insurrection; failure of French invasion
1804		Napoleon crowned Emperor
1805		Nelson dies at Trafalgar
1810	Southey, *The Curse of Kehama*	Mexican revolt against Spanish rule
1811		Prince of Wales becomes Prince Regent because of George III's insanity
1812	Byron, *Childe Harold's Pilgrimage*, I–II Humphry Davy, *Elements of Chemical Philosophy* Elgin Marbles arrive in London	Castlereagh becomes Foreign Secretary Spencer Perceval assassinated and replaced as Prime Minister by Lord Liverpool (till 1827) Napoleon begins retreat from Moscow
1813	Byron, *The Giaour* and *The Bride of Abydos*	Leigh and John Hunt imprisoned for libel on Prince Regent (till 1815)
1814	Byron, *The Corsair* Wordsworth, *The Excursion*	Congress of Vienna opens. Napoleon abdicates and is banished to Elba

Year	Age	Life

1815   23   Mary's first child born (22 Feb.); dies two weeks later.
Shelley receives annual income of £1,000 on death of
grandfather (June)

1816   24   Son William born to Mary (24 Jan.). *Alastor* published
(Feb.). With recently exiled Byron at Lake of Geneva,
where he writes 'Hymn to Intellectual Beauty' (late
June) and 'Mont Blanc' (late July) and Mary begins
Frankenstein (published 1818). Returns to England (8
Sept.); becomes friendly with Leigh Hunt. Suicide of
Mary's half-sister Fanny Imlay (9 Oct.). Suicide of
Harriet (9 Nov.). Marries Mary (30 Dec.)

1817   25   Birth of Allegra, Byron's daughter by Claire (12 Jan.).
Meets Keats (Feb.). Loses Ianthe and Charles through
judgement of Lord Eldon (27 Mar.). *Proposal for Putting
Reform to the Vote* published (Mar.). Daughter Clara born
(2 Sept.). *History of a Six Weeks' Tour* published. In bad
health. *An Address to the People on the Death of the
Princess Charlotte* published (written 11–12 Nov.) *Laon
and Cythna* published and withdrawn (Dec.)

1818   26   A more discreet version of *Laon and Cythna* published as
The Revolt of Islam (Jan.). Departs for Italy (11 Mar.).
Sends Allegra to Byron (28 Apr.). At Leghorn where he
meets John and Maria Gisborne and Maria's son Henry
Reveley. Visits Byron in Venice to discuss Allegra's
future (late Aug.), the inspiration for *Julian and Maddalo*;
settles at nearby Este till 5 Nov. Clara dies (24 Sept.).
Begins *Prometheus Unbound, Julian and Maddalo* and
'Lines Written among the Euganean Hills' (autumn).
Settles in Naples (11 Dec.). Visits Vesuvius, Bay of Baiae
and writes 'Stanzas Written in Dejection' (Dec.)

1819   27   Settles at Rome (5 Mar.), where he finishes Acts II and III
of *Prometheus Unbound* (Mar.–Apr.) William dies (7
June). Leaves Rome (10 June) and settles at Leghorn (17
June), where he works on *The Cenci*. Writes *The Mask of
Anarchy* (Sept.). Moves to Florence (2 Oct.); writes *Peter
Bell the Third* and 'Ode to the West Wind' (late Oct.).
Begins *A Philosophical View of Reform* (unfinished). Son
Percy Florence born (12 Nov.). 'England in 1819' (Dec.).
Birth (27 Dec.) of 'Elena Adelaide Shelley', Shelley's
'Neapolitan charge', registered as his own child by Mary
but of uncertain parentage (dies 9 June 1820)

Year	Artistic Events	Historical Events
1815	Schlegel, *Lectures on Dramatic Art and Literature* (translation)	Napoleon enters Paris, is defeated at Waterloo and exiled to St Helena
1816	Coleridge, *Christabel, Kubla Khan, The Pains of Sleep* Byron, *Childe Harold's Pilgrimage*, III Elgin Marbles purchased for British Museum	Spa Fields Riots in London after Reform meeting
1817	Byron, *Manfred* Coleridge, *Sibylline Leaves, Biographia Literaria* Keats, *Poems* Moore, *Lalla Rookh* Peacock, *Melincourt* Foundation of *Blackwood's Magazine*	Attack on Prince Regent. Habeas Corpus suspended (17 Mar.–31 Jan. 1818) after report of imminent insurrection; various measures against sedition. Derbyshire Riots
1818	Byron, *Beppo, Childe Harold*, IV Keats, *Endymion* Peacock, *Nightmare Abbey* Mary Shelley, *Frankenstein* Hunt, *Foliage* Moore, *Fudge Family in Paris*	Motion for parliamentary reform heavily defeated. Russia, Prussia, Britain and Austria renew Quadruple Alliance to protect France from revolutionary tendencies
1819	Byron, *Don Juan*, I–II Hunt, *The Indicator* Wordsworth, *Peter Bell*	'Peterloo' Massacre in Manchester after militia charges Reform meeting. Passing of the 'Six Acts', a series of strongly repressive measures

Year	Age	Life

1820   28   Moves to Pisa (Jan.). *The Cenci* published (spring). Moves to Leghorn (15 Jun.–4 Aug.). Writes 'The Sensitive-plant', 'Ode to Liberty' and 'The Cloud' (possibly at Pisa), 'To a Sky-lark' (probably June), *Letter to Maria Gisborne* (second half of June). At Baths of San Giuliano, near Pisa (Aug.–Oct.). Writes *The Witch of Atlas* (14–16 Aug.). *Promethus Unbound* published (Aug.). Returns to Pisa (31 Oct.). Friendship with Emilia Viviani (Dec.)

1821   29   Pirated edition of *Queen Mab* published in London. Working on *Epipsychidion* (finished 16 Feb.). Begins *A Defence of Poetry* in response to Peacock (Feb.-Mar.; not published till 1840). Hears of Keats's death in Rome on 23 Feb. (11 Apr.); writes *Adonais* (finished June; printed July). Anonymous publication of *Epipsychidion* (May). Visits Byron at Ravenna (Aug.). Writes *Hellas* (Oct.). Byron arrives at Pisa (Nov.)

1822   29   *Hellas* published (Feb.). Writes poems to Jane Williams; translates scenes from Goethe's *Faust* and Calderón (spring). Allegra Byron dies (20 Apr.). Moves to Casa Magni at San Terenzo near Lerici (30 Apr.). Sailing on the *Don Juan* (delivered 12 May). Writing *The Triumph of Life* (? late May–June; unfinished). Drowned when sailing back from Leghorn to Lerici after welcoming the Hunts (8 July)

1824   *Posthumous Poems* (collected by Mary from Shelley's papers)

Year	Artistic Events	Historical Events
1820	Keats, *Lamia, Isabella*, and *other Poems* Peacock, *The Four Ages of Poetry*	Beginnings of revolution in Spain. Discovery of Cato Street Conspiracy to murder Cabinet ministers. Death of George III, who is succeeded by Regent as George IV. Ferdinand VII restores Spanish Constitution and abolishes Inquisition. Revolt in Naples and promise of constitution. Bill of Pains and Penalties against Princess Caroline, whom George IV wishes to divorce, is introduced and dropped
1821	Byron, *The Prophecy of Dante*, *Don Juan*, III–IV	Greek War of Independence. Neapolitan rising crushed by Austrians, and Ferdinand IV restored. Death of Napoleon. Rejection of motion for parliamentary reform. Coronation of George IV and death of Caroline
1822		Greek independence proclaimed

Introduction

Percy Bysshe Shelley was born into a family with political connections. His father, Sir Timothy, was a Sussex landowner, a Whig MP attached to the liberal faction of the Duke of Norfolk; his liberalism did not extend to the behaviour of his own son, with whom he was permanently at odds after Shelley was sent down from Oxford in 1811 for refusing to acknowledge his authorship of an inquiring pamphlet called *The Necessity of Atheism*. Shelley had been intended to succeed his father in the House when he came of age; from his early years he was politically conscious, and his whole career was marked by a commitment to the possibilities of political reform which was both pragmatic and imaginative.

He grew up in that grim period sometimes known as the Bleak Age, the period of profound moral unrest and increasing political agitation which marked the years between the failure of the French Revolution and the passing of the Reform Bill in 1832. The first and perhaps the greatest influence on his political thinking was William Godwin, who later became his father-in-law. Godwin had imagined a utopian society in which there would be no need for government; much of Shelley's poetry, early and late, delights in presenting visions of a free and regenerated society, yet a growing sense of what was politically possible and a deeper understanding of human nature soon modified his belief in perfectibility. Shelley's main aim was to abolish the inequalities in society and to undermine the system of power and privilege on which they were based. In particular, this involved a reform of the electoral system, which currently excluded the vast majority of the population from the right to vote. The unfinished *A Philosophical View of Reform* (1819–? early 1820), intended to be 'an instructive and readable book, appealing from the passions to the reason of men', attracted no publisher but it is a shrewd and comprehensive account which places its subject in the context of European history. Shelley also attacked the unequal distribution of property; paper currency, the 'Ghost of Gold', whose consequences 'have been the establishment of a new aristocracy, which has its basis in fraud as the old one has its basis in force'; the operation of the National Debt; the use of the standing army; the legal system, including the barbaric Game Laws; and the rigid marriage laws which underestimated both the rights of women and the holiness of the heart's affections. Binding together all these abuses were the Church and the monarchy ('the only string which ties the robber's bundle'), who had combined themselves for their own benefit and to the 'destruction of the real interest of all'. Shelley crusaded with great energy: this infuses *Queen Mab* (1813), which was later known as 'the Chartists' Bible', and its supporting array of essays on social and political problems. It took Shelley to Dublin, where he addressed public meetings, distributed pamphlets and wrote his *Address to the Irish People*. It also animated the fiercely indignant *Address to the People on the Death of the Princess Charlotte* (1817) in which he drew attention to the way in which three leaders of a popular insurrection had been encouraged and betrayed by a government *agent provocateur*.

After he moved to Italy in the spring of 1818, Shelley became increasingly disillusioned both with direct political activity and with poetry which was bluntly didactic. Yet, when the situation demanded it, he could produce popular verse such as *The Mask of Anarchy*, which was specifically intended for a wide reading public. Poems like these were classed as *exoteric*; in his later years, Shelley preferred to concentrate on poetry of the *esoteric* species, aimed at the 'more select classes of poetical readers'. The aim was no longer simply didactic, but the predominating concerns were still moral and political. In *A Defence of Poetry* (written 1821) Shelley argued eloquently that poetry has an important social function; history shows that it is closely related to moral and social progress. In his own age the failure of the Industrial Revolution to increase the sum of human happiness could be attributed, along with the other excesses and imbalances of a capitalist economy, to a failure to 'imagine that which we know'. If man 'having enslaved the elements, remains himself a slave', it is because of 'an excess of the selfish and calculating principle' at the expense of imagination and its vehicle, poetry. The battle-lines are clearly drawn: 'Poetry and the principle of Self, of which money is the visible incarnation, are the God and Mammon of the world.'

Poetry is an act of hope; 'it is ever still the light of life; the source of whatever of beautiful or generous or true can have place in an evil time'. Shelley argues for the necessity of hope in the preface to

Laon and Cythna; or, The Revolution of the Golden City: A Vision of the Nineteenth Century (1817) (republished for reasons of discretion under the title *The Revolt of Islam*). There he claims that 'gloom and misanthropy have become the characteristics of the age in which we live, the solace of a disappointment that unconsciously finds relief only in the wilful exaggeration of its own despair'. Yet, in spite of the apparent failures of the high ideals of the French Revolution and the disillusionment and suffering of the Napoleonic Wars, the signs are that England has survived and that 'a slow, gradual silent change' is beginning to take place. *Laon and Cythna* was soon followed by *Prometheus Unbound* (written 1818–19, published 1820), a mythological drama which is perhaps Shelley's greatest achievement. The *Prometheus Bound* of Aeschylus had shown the archetypal revolutionary hero at odds with a tyrannical father-god; here Shelley provides a highly personal revisionary version and brings it to a conclusion which elicits its full potential for hope. In rewriting Aeschylus Shelley seems to have discovered new uses for Greek, Christian and Oriental mythology; the psychological profundity of his conception and the brilliantly daring imagery give to this play a satisfying complexity.

Even in his most optimistic works such as *Prometheus Unbound*, Shelley's idealism does not preclude some salutary examples of psychological realism; his hope was never naive or simple-minded. In other works, he argued against his own best inclinations: *Julian and Maddalo* presents a disillusioning reply to Julian's question 'if we were not weak / Should we be less in deed than in desire?', while Shelley's play *The Cenci* (intended for Covent Garden) portrays in Beatrice a character of Promethean potential who does not possess Prometheus' moral self-restraint, gives in to revenge and murders her father: 'all best things are thus confused to ill'. *Hellas*, which anticipates the success of the Greek War of Independence, begins its final chorus on a note of joyful celebration. Yet, before the chorus has ended, the joy has modulated into doubt: 'O cease! must hate and death return? / Cease! must men kill and die?'. Shelley delineated with grim precision the *danse macabre* of *The Triumph of Life* which includes sex as well as politics, literature and history; but he also wrote that 'Poetry is the record of the best and happiest moments of the happiest and best minds' and believed that 'Hope . . . is a solemn duty which we owe alike to ourselves & to the world'. It is part of his particular subtlety that he argues against himself within the confines of individual poems and that he also sets up poem against poem. The result is a continuous and fruitful dialectic, an energizing tension which gives force to most of his poetry.

One of Shelley's most distinctive literary achievements was his development of a richly symbolic poetry of mind which informs major poems such as 'Mont Blanc' and *Prometheus Unbound* as well as many of the shorter poems and lyrics such as 'The Sensitive-plant'. This draws on the 'peculiar style of intense and comprehensive imagery' which Shelley identified as distinguishing the 'modern literature of England'. He was thinking here of the poetic innovations of contemporaries such as Wordsworth, Coleridge and Byron (as well as the example of Greek literature) but his poetry was also driven by the restless psychological and philosophical curiosity which animated his own intellectual life. This interest can also be traced in a number of prose essays such as 'On Christianity' and 'On Life' in which Shelley grapples with fundamental issues concerning language, truth, religion and the nature of existence.

Shelley's poetry is also notable for the variety of its ambitions and accomplishments. Contrary to popular opinion, he was a poet not of one mode or style (the impassioned and lyrical) but of many. He could produce with equal skill and technical dexterity the learned formal ode in the high style ('Ode to Liberty'), the familiar verse epistle (*Letter to Maria Gisborne*), the satire (fiercely animated as in *The Mask of Anarchy* or more jocular as in *Peter Bell the Third*), the relaxed conversation poem (*Julian and Maddalo*), the Dantean history of love (*Epipsychidion*), the carefully wrought classical elegy (*Adonais*), the playful and liberated mythological fantasy (*The Witch of Atlas*), the extended exploratory lyric ('Lines Written in the Bay of Lerici') and the delighted celebration of natural energies ('The Cloud'). His descriptions of nature can range from the metaphysical analogies of 'Mont Blanc', to the precise but densely symbolic imagery of 'Ode to the West Wind', to the scientifically informed and imaginative visions of the earth and the moon in *Prometheus Unbound*, to the evocative landscape with which *Julian and Maddalo* begins. His voice can encompass the charming domestic detail ('We sate there rolling billiard balls about'), the compressed and paradoxical ('It is the unpastured Sea hungering for calm'), the profoundly philosophical ('The One remains, the many change and pass; / Heaven's light forever shines, Earth's shadows fly; / Life, like a dome of many-coloured glass, / Stains the white radiance of Eternity'), the bluntly comic ('He touched the hem of Nature's shift, / Felt faint – and never dared uplift / The closest, all-concealing tunic'), the grotesque ('His big tears, for he wept well, / Turned to millstones as they fell'), the morally incisive ('The good want power, but to weep barren tears. / The powerful goodness want: worse need for them. / The wise want love; and those who love want wisdom; / And all best things are thus confused to ill.' There is the ruthlessly unsentimental portrayal of sexual attraction in *The Triumph of Life*, the urbane conclusion to 'The Sensitive-plant', the joyful dance of the universe in Act IV of *Prometheus Unbound*, the gently chiding satire of 'An Exhortation', the pungently unsparing social and political analysis of 'England in 1819'. Such versatility goes a long way towards justifying Wordsworth's statement that 'Shelley is one of the best *artists* of us all: I mean in workmanship of style'.

This unusual capacity for variety and experiment presents a special challenge to the editor of a brief introductory selection. Unlike the case of Keats but rather like that of Byron, Shelley's best and most characteristic works cannot easily be represented in a hundred pages. It is tempting to concentrate on shorter poems, many of which are familiar or even famous. No satisfying and representative selection could afford to exclude poems such as 'Ozymandias' or 'Ode to the West Wind' or 'Lines Written in the Bay of Lerici' not to mention more complex personal and metaphysical explorations such as 'Mont Blanc', or fragments such as 'To the Moon' and 'O World, O Life, O Time'. Yet to focus exclusively on this area of Shelley's achievement would be to distort and undermine his even more compelling claim on our attention as the author of some of the most significant and original longer poems of the Romantic period, or perhaps of the whole nineteenth century. With a few exceptions (such as *Adonais*), these longer poems can only be represented here by extracts; some (such as *Queen Mab*, *Laon and Cythna* and *Alastor*) have had to be omitted altogether. The only feasible resolution is a series of extracts from the longer poems which is intended to be suggestive and stimulating rather than completely or exhaustively representative. Perhaps this selection may encourage readers not only to enjoy in their own right such intimations of a larger poetic achievement but also to embark on the even more rewarding challenge of reading the poems themselves.

TIMOTHY WEBB

Percy Bysshe Shelley

Hymn to Intellectual Beauty

1

The awful shadow of some unseen Power
    Floats though unseen amongst us, – visiting
    This various world with as inconstant wing
As summer winds that creep from flower to flower. –
Like moonbeams that behind some piny mountain shower,   5
      It visits with inconstant glance
      Each human heart and countenance;
Like hues and harmonies of evening, –
      Like clouds in starlight widely spread, –
      Like memory of music fled, –   10
      Like aught that for its grace may be
Dear, and yet dearer for its mystery.

2

Spirit of BEAUTY, that doth consecrate
    With thine own hues all thou dost shine upon
    Of human thought or form, – where art thou gone?   15
Why dost thou pass away and leave our state,
This dim vast vale of tears, vacant and desolate?
      Ask why the sunlight not forever
      Weaves rainbows o'er yon mountain river,
Why aught should fail and fade that once is shown,   20
      Why fear and dream and death and birth
      Cast on the daylight of this earth
      Such gloom, – why man has such a scope
For love and hate, despondency and hope?

3

No voice from some sublimer world hath ever   25
    To sage or poet these responses given –
    Therefore the name of God and ghosts and Heaven,
Remain the records of their vain endeavour,
Frail spells – whose uttered charm might not avail to sever
      From all we hear and all we see,   30

Doubt, chance and mutability.
Thy light alone – like mist o'er mountains driven,
    Or music by the night wind sent
    Through strings of some still instrument,
    Or moonlight on a midnight stream,   35
Gives grace and truth to life's unquiet dream.

4

Love, Hope, and Self-esteem, like clouds depart
    And come, for some uncertain moments lent.
    Man were immortal, and omnipotent,
Didst thou, unknown and awful as thou art,   40
Keep with thy glorious train firm state within his heart.
    Thou messenger of sympathies,
    That wax and wane in lovers' eyes –
Thou – that to human thought art nourishment,
    Like darkness to a dying flame!   45
    Depart not as thy shadow came,
    Depart not – lest the grave should be,
Like life and fear, a dark reality.

5

While yet a boy I sought for ghosts, and sped
    Through many a listening chamber, cave and ruin,   50
    And starlight wood, with fearful steps pursuing
Hopes of high talk with the departed dead.
I called on poisonous names with which our youth is fed,
    I was not heard – I saw them not –
    When musing deeply on the lot   55
Of life, at that sweet time when winds are wooing
    All vital things that wake to bring
    News of buds and blossoming, –
    Sudden, thy shadow fell on me;
I shrieked, and clasped my hands in ecstasy!   60

6

I vowed that I would dedicate my powers
    To thee and thine – have I not kept the vow?
    With beating heart and streaming eyes, even now
I call the phantoms of a thousand hours

Each from his voiceless grave: they have in visioned bowers
    Of studious zeal or love's delight   65
    Outwatched with me the envious night –
They know that never joy illumed my brow
    Unlinked with hope that thou wouldst free
    This world from its dark slavery,   70
    That thou – O awful LOVELINESS,
Wouldst give whate'er these words cannot express.

7

The day becomes more solemn and serene
  When noon is past – there is a harmony
  In autumn, and a lustre in its sky,   75
Which through the summer is not heard or seen,
As if it could not be, as if it had not been!
    Thus let thy power, which like the truth
    Of nature on my passive youth
Descended, to my onward life supply   80
    Its calm – to one who worships thee,
    And every form containing thee,
    Whom, SPIRIT fair, thy spells did bind
To fear himself, and love all human kind.

Mont Blanc

Lines Written in the Vale of Chamouni

1

The everlasting universe of things
Flows through the mind, and rolls its rapid waves,
Now dark – now glittering – now reflecting gloom –
Now lending splendour, where from secret springs
The source of human thought its tribute brings   5
Of waters, – with a sound but half its own,
Such as a feeble brook will oft assume

In the wild woods, among the mountains lone,
Where waterfalls around it leap forever,
Where woods and winds contend, and a vast river   10
Over its rocks ceaselessly bursts and raves.

                            2
Thus thou, Ravine of Arve – dark, deep Ravine –
Thou many-coloured, many-voicèd vale,
Over whose pines, and crags, and caverns sail
Fast cloud-shadows and sunbeams: awful scene,   15
Where Power in likeness of the Arve comes down
From the ice gulfs that gird his secret throne,
Bursting through these dark mountains like the flame
Of lightning through the tempest; – thou dost lie,
Thy giant brood of pines around thee clinging,   20
Children of elder time, in whose devotion
The chainless winds still come and ever came
To drink their odours, and their mighty swinging
To hear – an old and solemn harmony;
Thine earthly rainbows stretched across the sweep   25
Of the aethereal waterfall, whose veil
Robes some unsculptured image; the strange sleep
Which when the voices of the desert fail
Wraps all in its own deep eternity; –
Thy caverns echoing to the Arve's commotion,   30
A loud, lone sound no other sound can tame;
Thou art pervaded with that ceaseless motion,
Thou art the path of that unresting sound –
Dizzy Ravine! – and when I gaze on thee
I seem as in a trance sublime and strange   35
To muse on my own separate fantasy,
My own, my human mind, which passively
Now renders and receives fast influencings,
Holding an unremitting interchange
With the clear universe of things around;   40
One legion of wild thoughts, whose wandering wings
Now float above thy darkness, and now rest
Where that or thou art no unbidden guest,
In the still cave of the witch Poesy,
Seeking among the shadows that pass by,   45

Ghosts of all things that are, some shade of thee,
Some phantom, some faint image; till the breast
From which they fled recalls them, thou art there!

3

Some say that gleams of a remoter world
Visit the soul in sleep, — that death is slumber,   50
And that its shapes the busy thoughts outnumber
Of those who wake and live. — I look on high: —
Has some unknown omnipotence unfurled
The veil of life and death? or do I lie
In dream, and does the mightier world of sleep   55
Spread far around and inaccessibly
Its circles? For the very spirit fails,
Driven like a homeless cloud from steep to steep
That vanishes among the viewless gales!
Far, far above, piercing the infinite sky,   60
Mont Blanc appears, — still, snowy, and serene;
Its subject mountains their unearthly forms
Pile round it, ice and rock; broad vales between
Of frozen floods, unfathomable deeps,
Blue as the overhanging heaven, that spread   65
And wind among the accumulated steeps: —
A desert peopled by the storms alone,
Save when the eagle brings some hunter's bone,
And the wolf tracks her there — how hideously
Its shapes are heaped around! rude, bare, and high,   70
Ghastly, and scarred, and riven. — Is this the scene
Where the old Earthquake-daemon taught her young
Ruin? Were these their toys? or did a sea
Of fire envelop once this silent snow?
None can reply — all seems eternal now.   75
The wilderness has a mysterious tongue
Which teaches awful doubt, or faith so mild,
So solemn, so serene, that man may be
But for such faith with nature reconciled;
Thou hast a voice, great Mountain, to repeal   80
Large codes of fraud and woe; not understood
By all, but which the wise, and great, and good
Interpret, or make felt, or deeply feel.

4

The fields, the lakes, the forests, and the streams,
Ocean, and all the living things that dwell   85
Within the daedal earth; lightning, and rain,
Earthquake, and fiery flood, and hurricane,
The torpor of the year when feeble dreams
Visit the hidden buds, or dreamless sleep
Holds every future leaf and flower; – the bound   90
With which from that detested trance they leap;
The works and ways of man, their death and birth,
And that of him and all that his may be;
All things that move and breathe with toil and sound
Are born and die; revolve, subside and swell.   95
Power dwells apart in its tranquillity
Remote, serene, and inaccessible:
And *this*, the naked countenance of earth,
On which I gaze, even these primæval mountains
Teach the adverting mind. The glaciers creep   100
Like snakes that watch their prey, from their far fountains
Slow rolling on; there, many a precipice,
Frost and the Sun in scorn of mortal power
Have piled: dome, pyramid, and pinnacle,
A city of death, distinct with many a tower   105
And wall impregnable of beaming ice.
Yet not a city, but a flood of ruin
Is there, that from the boundaries of the sky
Rolls its perpetual stream; vast pines are strewing
Its destined path, or in the mangled soil   110
Branchless and shattered stand; the rocks, drawn down
From yon remotest waste, have overthrown
The limits of the dead and living world,
Never to be reclaimed. The dwelling-place
Of insects, beasts, and birds becomes its spoil;   115
Their food and their retreat forever gone,
So much of life and joy is lost. The race
Of man flies far in dread; his work and dwelling
Vanish, like smoke before the tempest's stream,
And their place is not known. Below, vast caves   120
Shine in the rushing torrents' restless gleam,

Which from those secret chasms in tumult welling
Meet in the vale, and one majestic River,
The breath and blood of distant lands, forever
Rolls its loud waters to the ocean waves,   125
Breathes its swift vapours to the circling air.

5

Mont Blanc yet gleams on high: – the power is there,
The still and solemn power of many sights,
And many sounds, and much of life and death.
In the calm darkness of the moonless nights,   130
In the lone glare of day, the snows descend
Upon that Mountain; none beholds them there,
Nor when the flakes burn in the sinking sun,
Or the star-beams dart through them. – Winds contend
Silently there, and heap the snow with breath   135
Rapid and strong, but silently! Its home
The voiceless lightning in these solitudes
Keeps innocently, and like vapour broods
Over the snow. The secret strength of things
Which governs thought, and to the infinite dome   140
Of heaven is as a law, inhabits thee!
And what were thou, and earth, and stars, and sea,
If to the human mind's imaginings
Silence and solitude were vacancy?

Ozymandias

I met a traveller from an antique land
Who said: 'Two vast and trunkless legs of stone
Stand in the desert. Near them, on the sand,
Half sunk, a shattered visage lies, whose frown,
And wrinkled lip, and sneer of cold command,   5
Tell that its sculptor well those passions read
Which yet survive, stamped on these lifeless things,

The hand that mocked them and the heart that fed;
And on the pedestal these words appear:
"My name is Ozymandias, king of kings: 10
Look on my works, ye Mighty, and despair!"
Nothing beside remains. Round the decay
Of that colossal wreck, boundless and bare
The lone and level sands stretch far away.'

Stanzas Written in Dejection – December 1818, near Naples

The Sun is warm, the sky is clear,
The waves are dancing fast and bright,
Blue isles and snowy mountains wear
The purple noon's transparent might,
The breath of the moist earth is light   5
Around its unexpanded buds;
Like many a voice of one delight
The winds, the birds, the Ocean-floods;
The City's voice itself is soft, like Solitude's.

I see the Deep's untrampled floor   10
With green and purple seaweeds strown,
I see the waves upon the shore
Like light dissolved in star-showers, thrown;
I sit upon the sands alone;
The lightning of the noontide Ocean   15
Is flashing round me, and a tone
Arises from its measured motion,
How sweet! did any heart now share in my emotion.

Alas, I have nor hope nor health,
Nor peace within nor calm around,   20
Nor that content surpassing wealth
The sage in meditation found,
And walked with inward glory crowned;

Nor fame nor power nor love nor leisure –
Others I see whom these surround,   25
Smiling they live and call life pleasure:
To me that cup has been dealt in another measure.

Yet now despair itself is mild,
Even as the winds and waters are;
I could lie down like a tired child   30
And weep away the life of care
Which I have borne and yet must bear,
Till Death like Sleep might steal on me,
And I might feel in the warm air
My cheek grow cold, and hear the Sea   35
Breathe o'er my dying brain its last monotony.

Some might lament that I were cold,
As I, when this sweet day is gone,
Which my lost heart, too soon grown old,
Insults with this untimely moan –   40
They might lament, – for I am one
Whom men love not, and yet regret;
Unlike this day, which, when the Sun
Shall on its stainless glory set,
Will linger, though enjoyed, like joy in memory yet.   45

from **Julian and Maddalo; A Conversation**

I rode one evening with Count Maddalo
Upon the bank of land which breaks the flow
Of Adria towards Venice: – a bare strand
Of hillocks, heaped from ever-shifting sand,
Matted with thistles and amphibious weeds,   5
Such as from earth's embrace the salt ooze breeds,
Is this; – an uninhabitable sea-side,
Which the lone fisher, when his nets are dried,
Abandons; and no other object breaks

The waste, but one dwarf tree and some few stakes   10
Broken and unrepaired, and the tide makes
A narrow space of level sand thereon,
Were 'twas our wont to ride while day went down.
This ride was my delight. – I love all waste
And solitary places; where we taste   15
The pleasure of believing what we see
Is boundless, as we wish our souls to be:
And such was this wide ocean, and this shore
More barren than its billows; – and yet more
Than all, with a remembered friend I love   20
To ride as then I rode; – for the winds drove
The living spray along the sunny air
Into our faces; the blue heavens were bare,
Stripped to their depths by the awakening North
And from the waves, sound like delight broke forth   25
Harmonizing with solitude, and sent
Into our hearts aërial merriment . . .
So, as we rode, we talked; and the swift thought,
Winging itself with laughter, lingered not
But flew from brain to brain, – such glee was ours –   30
Charged with light memories of remembered hours,
None slow enough for sadness; till we came
Homeward, which always makes the spirit tame.
This day had been cheerful but cold, and now
The sun was sinking, and the wind also.   35
Our talk grew somewhat serious, as may be
Talk interrupted with such raillery
As mocks itself, because it cannot scorn
The thoughts it would extinguish: – 'twas forlorn
Yet pleasing, such as once, so poets tell,   40
The devils held within the dales of Hell
Concerning God, freewill and destiny:
Of all that earth has been or yet may be,
All that vain men imagine or believe,
Or hope can paint or suffering may achieve,   45
We descanted, and I (for ever still
Is it not wise to make the best of ill?)
Argued against despondency, but pride
Made my companion take the darker side.

The sense that he was greater than his kind   50
Had struck, methinks, his eagle spirit blind
By gazing on its own exceeding light.
– Meanwhile the sun paused ere it should alight,
Over the horizon of the mountains; – Oh,
How beautiful is sunset, when the glow   55
Of Heaven descends upon a land like thee,
Thou Paradise of exiles, Italy!
Thy mountains, seas and vineyards and the towers
Of cities they encircle! – it was ours
To stand on thee, beholding it; and then   60
Just where we had dismounted, the Count's men
Were waiting for us with the gondola. –
As those who pause on some delightful way
Though bent on pleasant pilgrimage, we stood
Looking upon the evening and the flood   65
Which lay between the city and the shore
Paved with the image of the sky . . . the hoar
And aery Alps towards the North appeared
Through mist, an heaven-sustaining bulwark reared
Between the East and West; and half the sky   70
Was roofed with clouds of rich emblazonry
Dark purple at the zenith, which still grew
Down the steep West into a wondrous hue
Brighter than burning gold, even to the rent
Where the swift sun yet paused in his descent   75
Among the many-folded hills: they were
Those famous Euganean hills, which bear
As seen from Lido through the harbour piles
The likeness of a clump of peakèd isles –
And then – as if the Earth and Sea had been   80
Dissolved into one lake of fire, were seen
Those mountains towering as from waves of flame
Around the vaporous sun, from which there came
The inmost purple spirit of light, and made
Their very peaks transparent. 'Ere it fade,'   85
Said my companion, 'I will show you soon
A better station' – so, o'er the lagoon
We glided, and from that funereal bark
I leaned, and saw the city, and could mark

How from their many isles in evening's gleam   90
Its temples and its palaces did seem
Like fabrics of enchantment piled to Heaven.
I was about to speak, when – 'We are even
Now at the point I meant,' said Maddalo,
And bade the gondolieri cease to row.   95
'Look, Julian, on the west, and listen well
If you hear not a deep and heavy bell.'
I looked, and saw between us and the sun
A building on an island; such a one
As age to age might add, for uses vile,   100
A windowless, deformed and dreary pile,
And on the top an open tower, where hung
A bell, which in the radiance swayed and swung –
We could just hear its hoarse and iron tongue:
The broad sun sunk behind it, and it tolled   105
In strong and black relief. – 'What we behold
Shall be the madhouse and its belfry tower,'
Said Maddalo, 'and ever at this hour
Those who may cross the water, hear that bell
Which calls the maniacs each one from his cell   110
To vespers.' – 'As much skill as need to pray
In thanks or hope for their dark lot have they
To their stern maker,' I replied. 'O ho!
You talk as in years past,' said Maddalo.
''Tis strange men change not. You were ever still   115
Among Christ's flock a perilous infidel,
A wolf for the meek lambs – if you can't swim
Beware of Providence.' I looked on him,
But the gay smile had faded in his eye:
'And such,' – he cried, 'is our mortality   120
And this must be the emblem and the sign
Of what should be eternal and divine! –
And like that black and dreary bell, the soul,
Hung in a heaven-illumined tower, must toll
Our thoughts and our desires to meet below   125
Round the rent heart and pray – as madmen do
For what? they know not, – till the night of death
As sunset that strange vision, severeth
Our memory from itself, and us from all

We sought and yet were baffled!' I recall   130
The sense of what he said, although I mar
The force of his expressions. The broad star
Of day meanwhile had sunk behind the hill
And the black bell became invisible
And the red tower looked grey, and all between   135
The churches, ships and palaces were seen
Huddled in gloom; – into the purple sea
The orange hues of heaven sunk silently.
We hardly spoke, and soon the gondola
Conveyed me to my lodging by the way.   140

    The following morn was rainy, cold and dim:
Ere Maddalo arose, I called on him,
And whilst I waited with his child I played;
A lovelier toy sweet Nature never made,
A serious, subtle, wild, yet gentle being,   145
Graceful without design and unforeseeing,
With eyes – oh speak not of her eyes! – which seem
Twin mirrors of Italian Heaven, yet gleam
With such deep meaning, as we never see
But in the human countenance: with me   150
She was a special favourite: I had nursed
Her fine and feeble limbs when she came first
To this bleak world; and she yet seemed to know
On second sight her ancient playfellow,
Less changed than she was by six months or so;   155
For after her first shyness was worn out
We sate there, rolling billiard balls about.
When the Count entered – salutations past –
'The words you spoke last night might well have cast
A darkness on my spirit – if man be   160
The passive thing you say, I should not see
Much harm in the religions and old saws
(Though I may never own such leaden laws)
Which break a teachless nature to the yoke:
Mine is another faith' – thus much I spoke,   165
And noting he replied not, added: 'See
This lovely child, blithe, innocent and free;
She spends a happy time with little care

While we to such sick thoughts subjected are
As came on you last night – it is our will   170
That thus enchains us to permitted ill –
We might be otherwise – we might be all
We dream of happy, high, majestical.
Where is the love, beauty and truth we seek
But in our mind? and if we were not weak   175
Should we be less in deed than in desire?'
'Aye, if we were not weak – and we aspire
How vainly to be strong!' said Maddalo:
'You talk Utopia.' 'It remains to know,'
I then rejoined, 'and those who try may find   180
How strong the chains are which our spirit bind;
Brittle perchance as straw . . . We are assured
Much may be conquered, much may be endured
Of what degrades and crushes us. We know
That we have power over ourselves to do   185
And suffer – what, we know not till we try;
But something nobler than to live and die –
So taught those kings of old philosophy
Who reigned, before Religion made men blind;
And those who suffer with their suffering kind   190
Yet feel their faith, religion.' 'My dear friend,'
Said Maddalo, 'my judgement will not bend
To your opinion, though I think you might
Make such a system refutation-tight
As far as words go. I knew one like you   195
Who to this city came some months ago
With whom I argued in this sort, and he
Is now gone mad, – and so he answered me, –
Poor fellow! but if you would like to go
We'll visit him, and his wild talk will show   200
How vain are such aspiring theories.'
'I hope to prove the induction otherwise,
And that a want of that true theory, still
Which seeks a "soul of goodness" in things ill
Or in himself or others has thus bowed
His being – there are some by nature proud,   205
Who patient in all else demand but this:
To love and be beloved with gentleness;

And being scorned, what wonder if they die
Some living death? this is not destiny 210
But man's own wilfull ill.' As thus I spoke,
Servants announced the gondola, and we
Through the fast-falling rain and high-wrought sea
Sailed to the island where the madhouse stands.
We disembarked. The clap of tortured hands, 215
Fierce yells and howlings and lamentings keen,
And laughter where complaint had merrier been,
Moans, shrieks and curses and blaspheming prayers
Accosted us. We climbed the oozy stairs
Into an old courtyard. I heard on high, 220
Then, fragments of most touching melody
But looking up saw not the singer there –
Through the black bars in the tempestuous air
I saw, like weeds on a wrecked palace growing,
Long tangled locks flung wildly forth, and flowing, 225
Of those who on a sudden were beguiled
Into strange silence, and looked forth and smiled
Hearing sweet sounds. – Then I: 'Methinks there were
A cure of these with patience and kind care,
If music can thus move . . . but what is he 230
Whom we seek here?' 'Of his sad history
I know but this,' said Maddalo: 'he came
To Venice a dejected man, and fame
Said he was wealthy, or he had been so;
Some thought the loss of fortune wrought him woe; 235
But he was ever talking in such sort
As you do – far more sadly – he seemed hurt,
Even as a man with his peculiar wrong,
To hear but of the oppression of the strong,
Or those absurd deceits (I think with you 240
In some respects, you know) which carry through
The excellent impostors of this earth
When they outface detection – he had worth,
Poor fellow! but a humourist in his way' –
'Alas, what drove him mad?' 'I cannot say: 245
A lady came with him from France, and when
She left him and returned, he wandered then
About yon lonely isles of desert sand

Till he grew wild – he had no cash or land
Remaining, – the police had brought him here –   250
Some fancy took him and he would not bear
Removal; so I fitted up for him
Those rooms beside the sea, to please his whim,
And sent him busts and books and urns for flowers
Which had adorned his life in happier hours,   255
And instruments of music – you may guess
A stranger could do little more or less
For one so gentle and unfortunate,
And those are his sweet strains which charm the weight
From madmen's chains, and make this Hell appear   260
A heaven of sacred silence, hushed to hear.' –
'Nay, this was kind of you – he had no claim,
As the world says' – 'None – but the very same
Which I on all mankind were I as he
Fallen to such deep reverse; – his melody   265
Is interrupted now – we hear the din
Of madmen, shriek on shriek again begin;
Let us now visit him; after this strain
He ever communes with himself again,
And sees nor hears not any.' Having said   270
These words we called the keeper, and he led
To an apartment opening on the sea –
There the poor wretch was sitting mournfully
Near a piano, his pale fingers twined
One with the other, and the ooze and wind   275
Rushed through an open casement, and did sway
His hair, and starred it with the brackish spray;
His head was leaning on a music book,
And he was muttering, and his lean limbs shook;
His lips were pressed against a folded leaf   280
In hue too beautiful for health, and grief
Smiled in their motions as they lay apart –
As one who wrought from his own fervid heart
The eloquence of passion, soon he raised
His sad meek face and eyes lustrous and glazed   285
And spoke – sometimes as one who wrote and thought
His words might move some heart that heeded not
If sent to distant lands: and then as one

Reproaching deeds never to be undone
With wondering self-compassion; then his speech   290
Was lost in grief, and then his words came each
Unmodulated, cold, expressionless;
But that from one jarred accent you might guess
It was despair made them so uniform:
And all the while the loud and gusty storm   295
Hissed through the window, and we stood behind
Stealing his accents from the envious wind
Unseen. I yet remember what he said
Distinctly: such impression his words made.

'Month after month,' he cried, 'to bear this load   300
And as a jade urged by the whip and goad
To drag life on, which like a heavy chain
Lengthens behind with many a link of pain! –
And not to speak my grief – o not to dare
To give a human voice to my despair   305
But live and move, and wretched thing! smile on
As if I never went aside to groan
And wear this mask of falsehood even to those
Who are most dear – not for my own repose –
Alas, no scorn or pain or hate could be   310
So heavy as that falsehood is to me –
But that I cannot bear more altered faces
Than needs must be, more changed and cold embraces,
More misery, disappointment and mistrust
To own me for their father . . . Would the dust   315
Were covered in upon my body now!
That the life ceased to toil within my brow!
And then these thoughts would at the least be fled;
Let us not fear such pain can vex the dead.

'What Power delights to torture us? I know   320
That to myself I do not wholly owe
What now I suffer, though in part I may.
Alas, none strewed sweet flowers upon the way
Where wandering heedlessly, I met pale Pain,
My shadow, which will leave me not again –   325
If I have erred, there was no joy in error,

But pain and insult and unrest and terror;
I have not as some do, bought penitence
With pleasure, and a dark yet sweet offence,
For then, – if love and tenderness and truth   330
Had overlived hope's momentary youth,
My creed should have redeemed me from repenting;
But loathèd scorn and outrage unrelenting
Met love excited by far other seeming
Until the end was gained . . . as one from dreaming   335
Of sweetest peace, I woke, and found my state
Such as it is. –

        'O thou, my spirit's mate
Who, for thou art compassionate and wise,
Wouldst pity me from thy most gentle eyes
If this sad writing thou shouldst ever see –   340
My secret groans must be unheard by thee,
Thou wouldst weep tears bitter as blood to know
Thy lost friend's incommunicable woe.

.   .   .   .

            'Alas, love,
Fear me not . . . against thee I would not move
A finger in despite. Do I not live
That thou mayst have less bitter cause to grieve?   495
I give thee tears for scorn and love for hate;
And that thy lot may be less desolate
Than his on whom thou tramplest, I refrain
From that sweet sleep which medicines all pain.
Then, when thou speakest of me, never say   500
"He could forgive not." Here I cast away
All human passions, all revenge, all pride;
I think, speak, act no ill; I do but hide
Under these words like embers, every spark
Of that which has consumed me – quick and dark   505
The grave is yawning . . . as its roof shall cover
My limbs with dust and worms under and over
So let Oblivion hide this grief . . . the air
Closes upon my accents, as despair
Upon my heart – let death upon despair!'   510

He ceased, and overcome leant back awhile,
Then rising, with a melancholy smile
Went to a sofa, and lay down, and slept
A heavy sleep, and in his dreams he wept   515
And muttered some familiar name, and we
Wept without shame in his society.
I think I never was impressed so much;
The man who were not, must have lacked a touch
Of human nature . . . then we lingered not,   520
Although our argument was quite forgot,
But calling the attendants, went to dine
At Maddalo's; yet neither cheer nor wine
Could give us spirits, for we talked of him
And nothing else, till daylight made stars dim;
And we agreed his was some dreadful ill   525
Wrought on him boldly, yet unspeakable,
By a dear friend; some deadly change in love
Of one vowed deeply which he dreamed not of;
For whose sake he, it seemed, had fixed a blot
Of falsehood on his mind which flourished not   530
But in the light of all-beholding truth;
And having stamped this canker on his youth
She had abandoned him – and how much more
Might be his woe, we guessed not – he had store
Of friends and fortune once, as we could guess   535
From his nice habits and his gentleness;
These were now lost . . . it were a grief indeed
If he had changed one unsustaining reed
For all that such a man might else adorn.
The colours of his mind seemed yet unworn;   540
For the wild language of his grief was high,
Such as in measure were called poetry;
And I remember one remark which then
Maddalo made. He said: 'Most wretched men
Are cradled into poetry by wrong,   545
They learn in suffering what they teach in song.'

If I had been an unconnected man
I, from this moment, should have formed some plan
Never to leave sweet Venice, – for to me

It was delight to ride by the lone sea;   550
And then, the town is silent – one may write
Or read in gondolas by day or night,
Having the little brazen lamp alight,
Unseen, uninterrupted; books are there,
Pictures, and casts from all those statues fair   555
Which were twin-born with poetry, and all
We seek in towns, with little to recall
Regrets for the green country. I might sit
In Maddalo's great palace, and his wit
And subtle talk would cheer the winter night   560
And make me know myself, and the firelight
Would flash upon our faces, till the day
Might dawn and make me wonder at my stay:
But I had friends in London too: the chief
Attraction here, was that I sought relief   565
From the deep tenderness that maniac wrought
Within me – 'twas perhaps an idle thought,
But I imagined that if day by day
I watched him, and but seldom went away,
And studied all the beatings of his heart   570
With zeal, as men study some stubborn art
For their own good, and could by patience find
An entrance to the caverns of his mind,
I might reclaim him from his dark estate:
In friendships I had been most fortunate –   575
Yet never saw I one whom I would call
More willingly my friend; and this was all
Accomplished not; such dreams of baseless good
Oft come and go in crowds or solitude
And leave no trace – but what I now designed   580
Made for long years impression on my mind.
The following morning urged by my affairs
I left bright Venice.

              After many years
And many changes I returned; the name
Of Venice, and its aspect, was the same;   585
But Maddalo was travelling far away

Among the mountains of Armenia.
His dog was dead. His child had now become
A woman; such as it has been my doom
To meet with few, – a wonder of this earth   590
Where there is little of transcendent worth, –
Like one of Shakespeare's women: kindly she
And with a manner beyond courtesy
Received her father's friend; and when I asked
Of the lorn maniac, she her memory tasked   595
And told as she had heard the mournful tale:
'That the poor sufferer's health began to fail
Two years from my departure, but that then
The lady who had left him, came again.
Her mien had been imperious, but she now   600
Looked meek – perhaps remorse had brought her low.
Her coming made him better, and they stayed
Together at my father's – for I played
As I remember with the lady's shawl –
I might be six years old – but after all   605
She left him' . . . 'Why, her heart must have been tough:
How did it end?' 'And was not this enough?
They met – they parted' – 'Child, is there no more?'
'Something within that interval which bore
The stamp of *why* they parted, *how* they met; –   610
Yet if thine agèd eyes disdain to wet
Those wrinkled cheeks with youth's remembered tears,
Ask me no more, but let the silent years
Be closed and ceared over their memory
As yon mute marble where their corpses lie.'   615
I urged and questioned still, she told me how
All happened – but the cold world shall not know.

from **Prometheus Unbound:**
A Lyrical Drama in Four Acts

Ione.   Even whilst we speak
New notes arise. What is that awful sound?
   Panthea. 'Tis the deep music of the rolling world
Kindling within the strings of the waved air
Æolian modulations.
   Ione.   Listen too,   5
How every pause is filled with under-notes,
Clear, silver, icy, keen, awakening tones,
Which pierce the sense, and live within the soul,
As the sharp stars pierce winter's crystal air
And gaze upon themselves within the sea.   10
   Panthea. But see where through two openings in the forest
Which hanging branches overcanopy,
And where two runnels of a rivulet,
Between the close moss violet-inwoven,
Have made their path of melody, like sisters   15
Who part with sighs that they may meet in smiles,
Turning their dear disunion to an isle
Of lovely grief, a wood of sweet sad thoughts;
Two visions of strange radiance float upon
The ocean-like enchantment of strong sound,   20
Which flows intenser, keener, deeper yet
Under the ground and through the windless air.
   Ione. I see a chariot like that thinnest boat,
In which the Mother of the Months is borne
By ebbing light into her western cave,   25
When she upsprings from interlunar dreams;
O'er which is curved an orblike canopy
Of gentle darkness, and the hills and woods,
Distinctly seen through that dusk aery veil,
Regard like shapes in an enchanter's glass;   30
Its wheels are solid clouds, azure and gold,
Such as the genii of the thunderstorm
Pile on the floor of the illumined sea
When the sun rushes under it; they roll
And move and grow as with an inward wind;   35

Within it sits a wingèd infant, white
Its countenance, like the whiteness of bright snow,
Its plumes are as feathers of sunny frost,
Its limbs gleam white, through the wind-flowing folds
Of its white robe, woof of ethereal pearl.   40
Its hair is white, the brightness of white light
Scattered in strings; yet its two eyes are heavens
Of liquid darkness, which the Deity
Within seems pouring, as a storm is poured
From jaggèd clouds, out of their arrowy lashes,   45
Tempering the cold and radiant air around,
With fire that is not brightness; in its hand
It sways a quivering moonbeam, from whose point
A guiding power directs the chariot's prow
Over its wheelèd clouds, which as they roll   50
Over the grass, and flowers, and waves, wake sounds,
Sweet as a singing rain of silver dew.
    Panthea. And from the other opening in the wood
Rushes, with loud and whirlwind harmony,
A sphere, which is as many thousand spheres,   55
Solid as crystal, yet through all its mass
Flow, as through empty space, music and light:
Ten thousand orbs involving and involved,
Purple and azure, white, and green, and golden,
Sphere within sphere; and every space between   60
Peopled with unimaginable shapes,
Such as ghosts dream dwell in the lampless deep,
Yet each intertranspicuous, and they whirl
Over each other with a thousand motions,
Upon a thousand sightless axles spinning,   65
And with the force of self-destroying swiftness,
Intensely, slowly, solemnly roll on,
Kindling with mingled sounds, and many tones,
Intelligible words and music wild.
With mighty whirl the multitudinous orb   70
Grinds the bright brook into an azure mist
Of elemental subtlety, like light;
And the wild odour of the forest flowers,
The music of the living grass and air,
The emerald light of leaf-entangled beams   75

Round its intense yet self-conflicting speed,
Seem kneaded into the aëreal mass
Which drowns the sense. Within the orb itself,
Pillowed upon its alabaster arms,
Like to a child o'erwearied with sweet toil,   80
On its own folded wings, and wavy hair,
The Spirit of the Earth is laid asleep,
And you can see its little lips are moving,
Amid the changing light of their own smiles,
Like one who talks of what he loves in dream.   85
   Ione. 'Tis only mocking the orb's harmony . . .
   Panthea. And from a star upon its forehead, shoot,
Like swords of azure fire, or golden spears
With tyrant-quelling myrtle overtwined,
Embleming heaven and earth united now,   90
Vast beams like spokes of some invisible wheel
Which whirl as the orb whirls, swifter than thought,
Filling the abyss with sun-like lightenings,
And perpendicular now, and now transverse,
Pierce the dark soil, and as they pierce and pass,   95
Make bare the secrets of the earth's deep heart;
Infinite mines of adamant and gold,
Valueless stones, and unimagined gems,
And caverns on crystalline columns poised
With vegetable silver overspread;   100
Wells of unfathomed fire, and water springs
Whence the great sea, even as a child is fed,
Whose vapours clothe earth's monarch mountain-tops
With kingly, ermine snow. The beams flash on
And make appear the melancholy ruins   105
Of cancelled cycles; anchors, beaks of ships;
Planks turned to marble; quivers, helms, and spears,
And gorgon-headed targes, and the wheels
Of scythèd chariots, and the emblazonry
Of trophies, standards, and armorial beasts,   110
Round which death laughed, sepulchred emblems
Of dead destruction, ruin within ruin!
The wrecks beside of many a city vast,
Whose population which the earth grew over
Was mortal, but not human; see, they lie,   115

Their monstrous works, and uncouth skeletons,
Their statues, homes and fanes; prodigious shapes
Huddled in gray annihilation, split,
Jammed in the hard, black deep; and over these,
The anatomies of unknown wingèd things,   120
And fishes which were isles of living scale,
And serpents, bony chains, twisted around
The iron crags, or within heaps of dust
To which the tortuous strength of their last pangs
Had crushed the iron crags; and over these   125
The jaggèd alligator, and the might
Of earth-convulsing behemoth, which once
Were monarch beasts, and on the slimy shores,
And weed-overgrown continents of earth,
Increased and multiplied like summer worms   130
On an abandoned corpse, till the blue globe
Wrapped deluge round it like a cloak, and they
Yelled, gasped, and were abolished; or some God
Whose throne was in a comet, passed, and cried,
'Be not!' And like my words they were no more.   135

The Mask of Anarchy Written on the Occasion of the Massacre at Manchester

As I lay asleep in Italy
There came a voice from over the Sea,
And with great power it forth led me
To walk in the Visions of Poesy.

I met Murder on the way –   5
He had a mask like Castlereagh,
Very smooth he looked, yet grim;
Seven bloodhounds followed him:

All were fat; and well they might
Be in admirable plight,   10

For one by one, and two by two,
He tossed them human hearts to chew
Which from his wide cloak he drew.

Next came Fraud, and he had on,
Like Eldon, an erminèd gown;   15
His big tears, for he wept well,
Turned to mill-stones as they fell,

And the little children who
Round his feet played to and fro,
Thinking every tear a gem,   20
Had their brains knocked out by them.

Clothed with the Bible, as with light,
And the shadows of the night,
Like Sidmouth next, Hypocrisy
On a crocodile rode by.   25

And many more Destructions played
In this ghastly masquerade,
All disguised, even to the eyes,
Like Bishops, lawyers, peers or spies.

Last came Anarchy: he rode   30
On a white horse, splashed with blood;
He was pale even to the lips,
Like Death in the Apocalypse.

And he wore a kingly crown;
And in his grasp a sceptre shone;   35
On his brow this mark I saw –
'I AM GOD AND KING AND LAW.'

With a pace stately and fast,
Over English land he passed,
Trampling to a mire of blood   40
The adoring multitude.

And a mighty troop around,
With their trampling shook the ground,

Waving each a bloody sword,
For the service of their Lord;   45

And with glorious triumph, they
Rode through England proud and gay,
Drunk as with intoxication
Of the wine of desolation.

O'er fields and towns, from sea to sea,   50
Passed that Pageant swift and free,
Tearing up and trampling down
Till they came to London town;

And each dweller, panic-stricken,
Felt his heart with terror sicken   55
Hearing the tempestuous cry
Of the triumph of Anarchy.

For with pomp to meet him came
Clothed in arms like blood and flame
The hired Murderers, who did sing   60
'Thou art God and Law and King.

'We have waited weak and lone
For thy coming, Mighty One!
Our purses are empty, our swords are cold,
Give us glory and blood and gold.'   65

Lawyers and priests, a motley crowd,
To the Earth their pale brows bowed,
Like a bad prayer not overloud
Whispering – 'Thou art Law and God.'

Then all cried with one accord   70
'Thou art King and God and Lord;
Anarchy, to Thee we bow,
Be Thy name made holy now!'

And Anarchy, the Skeleton,
Bowed and grinned to every one,   75

As well as if his education
Had cost ten millions to the Nation.

For he knew the Palaces
Of our Kings were rightly his;
His the sceptre, crown and globe,   80
And the gold-inwoven robe.

So he sent his slaves before
To seize upon the Bank and Tower,
And was proceeding with intent
To meet his pensioned Parliament   85

When One fled past, a Maniac maid,
And her name was Hope, she said:
But she looked more like Despair,
And she cried out in the air –

'My father Time is weak and grey   90
With waiting for a better day –
See how idiot-like he stands
Fumbling with his palsied hands!

'He has had child after child
And the dust of death is piled   95
Over every one but me –
Misery, o Misery!'

Then she lay down in the street
Right before the horses' feet,
Expecting with a patient eye   100
Murder, Fraud and Anarchy,

When between her and her foes
A mist, a light, an image rose,
Small at first, and weak and frail
Like the vapour of a vale,   105

Till as clouds grow on the blast
Like tower-crowned giants striding fast,

And glare with lightnings as they fly
And speak in thunder to the sky,

It grew – a Shape arrayed in mail   110
Brighter than the viper's scale,
And upborne on wings whose grain
Was as the light of sunny rain.

On its helm seen far away
A planet, like the Morning's lay;   115
And those plumes its light rained through
Like a shower of crimson dew;

With step as soft as wind it passed
O'er the heads of men – so fast
That they knew the presence there   120
And looked – but all was empty air.

As flowers beneath May's footstep waken,
As stars from Night's loose hair are shaken,
As waves arise when loud winds call,
Thoughts sprung where'er that step did fall.   125

And the prostrate multitude
Looked – and ankle-deep in blood
Hope, that maiden most serene,
Was walking with a quiet mien,

And Anarchy, the ghastly birth,   130
Lay dead earth upon the earth –
The Horse of Death tameless as wind
Fled, and with his hoofs did grind
To dust the murderers thronged behind.

A rushing light of clouds and splendour,   135
A sense awakening and yet tender
Was heard and felt – and at its close
These words of joy and fear arose

As if their own indignant Earth
Which gave the Sons of England birth   140
Had felt their blood upon her brow,
And shuddering with a mother's throe

Had turned every drop of blood
By which her face had been bedewed
To an accent unwithstood –   145
As if her heart cried out aloud:

'Men of England, Heirs of Glory,
Heroes of unwritten Story,
Nurslings of one mighty Mother,
Hopes of her and one another,   150

'Rise like Lions after slumber
In unvanquishable number,
Shake your chains to Earth like dew
Which in sleep had fallen on you –
Ye are many – they are few.   155

'What is Freedom? – ye can tell
That which slavery is, too well –
For its very name has grown
To an echo of your own.

''Tis to work and have such pay   160
As just keeps life from day to day
In your limbs, as in a cell
For the tyrants' use to dwell,

'So that ye for them are made
Loom and plough and sword and spade,   165
With or without your own will bent
To their defence and nourishment;

''Tis to see your children weak
With their mothers pine and peak
When the winter winds are bleak –   170
They are dying whilst I speak;

''Tis to hunger for such diet
As the rich man in his riot
Casts to the fat dogs that lie
Surfeiting beneath his eye;   175

''Tis to let the Ghost of Gold
Take from Toil a thousandfold
More than e'er its substance could
In the tyrannies of old –

'Paper coin, that forgery   180
Of the title deeds, which ye
Hold to something from the worth
Of the inheritance of Earth;

''Tis to be a slave in soul
And to hold no strong control   185
Over your own will, but be
All that others make of ye;

'And at length when ye complain
With a murmur weak and vain,
'Tis to see the tyrants' crew   190
Ride over your wives and you –
Blood is on the grass like dew.

'Then it is to feel revenge
Fiercely thirsting to exchange
Blood for blood, and wrong for wrong –   195
Do not thus when ye are strong.

'Birds find rest, in narrow nest
When weary of their wingèd quest,
Beasts find fare, in woody lair
When storm and snow are in the air;   200

'Horses, oxen, have a home
When from daily toil they come;
Household dogs, when the wind roars
Find a home within warm doors;

'Asses, swine, have litter spread   205
And with fitting food are fed;
All things have a home but one –
Thou, o Englishman, hast none!

'This is slavery – savage men
Or wild beasts within a den   210
Would endure not as ye do –
But such ills they never knew.

'What art thou, Freedom? o, could slaves
Answer from their living graves
This demand, tyrants would flee   215
Like a dream's dim imagery.

'Thou art not as imposters say
A Shadow soon to pass away,
A Superstition, and a name
Echoing from the cave of Fame: 220

'For the labourer thou art bread
And a comely table spread,
From his daily labour come,
In a neat and happy home;

'Thou art clothes and fire and food   225
For the trampled multitude –
No – in countries that are free
Such starvation cannot be
As in England now we see.

'To the rich thou art a check –   230
When his foot is on the neck
Of his victim, thou dost make
That he treads upon a snake.

'Thou art Justice – ne'er for gold
May thy righteous laws be sold
As laws are in England – thou   235
Shieldst alike both high and low.

'Thou art Wisdom – Freemen never
Dream that God will damn forever
All who think those things untrue   240
Of which Priests make such ado.

'Thou art Peace – never by thee
Would blood and treasure wasted be
As tyrants wasted them, when all
Leagued to quench thy flame in Gaul.   245

'What if English toil and blood
Was poured forth even as a flood?
It availed, o Liberty,
To dim, but not extinguish thee.

'Thou art Love – the rich have kissed   250
Thy feet, and like him following Christ
Give their substance to the free
And through the rough world follow thee,

'Or turn their wealth to arms, and make
War for thy belovèd sake   255
On wealth and war and fraud – whence they
Drew the power which is their prey.

'Science, Poetry and Thought
Are thy lamps; they make the lot
Of the dwellers in a cot   260
Such, they curse their Maker not.

'Spirit, Patience, Gentleness,
All that can adorn and bless
Art thou . . . let deeds not words express
Thine exceeding loveliness –   265

'Let a great Assembly be
Of the fearless and the free
On some spot of English ground
Where the plains stretch wide around.

'Let the blue sky overhead,   270
The green earth on which ye tread,
All that must eternal be
Witness the Solemnity.

'From the corners uttermost
Of the bounds of English coast,   275
From every hut, village and town
Where those who live and suffer, moan
For others' misery or their own –

'From the workhouse and the prison
Where pale as corpses newly risen   280
Women, children, young and old
Groan for pain and weep for cold –

'From the haunts of daily life
Where is waged the daily strife
With common wants and common cares   285
Which sows the human heart with tares –

'Lastly from the palaces
Where the murmur of distress
Echoes, like the distant sound
Of a wind alive around   290

'Those prison-halls of wealth and fashion
Where some few feel such compassion
For those who groan and toil and wail
As must make their brethren pale,

'Ye who suffer woes untold   295
Or to feel or to behold
Your lost country bought and sold
With a price of blood and gold –

'Let a vast Assembly be,
And with great solemnity   300
Declare with measured words that ye
Are, as God has made ye, free –

'Be your strong and simple words
Keen to wound as sharpened swords,
And wide as targes let them be   *shield*   305
With their shade to cover ye.

'Let the tyrants pour around
With a quick and startling sound
Like the loosening of a sea
Troops of armed emblazonry.   310

'Let the charged artillery drive
Till the dead air seems alive
With the clash of clanging wheels
And the tramp of horses' heels.

'Let the fixèd bayonet   315
Gleam with sharp desire to wet
Its bright point in English blood –
Looking keen. as one for food.

'Let the horsemen's scimitars
Wheel and flash like sphereless stars   320
Thirsting to eclipse their burning
In a sea of death and mourning.

'Stand ye calm and resolute
Like a forest close and mute
With folded arms and looks which are   325
Weapons of unvanquished war,

'And let Panic who outspeeds
The career of armed steeds
Pass, a disregarded shade,
Through your phalanx undismayed.   330

'Let the Laws of your own land,
Good or ill, between ye stand
Hand to hand and foot to foot,
Arbiters of the dispute,

'The old laws of England – they   335
Whose reverend heads with age are grey,
Children of a wiser day,
And whose solemn voice must be
Thine own echo – Liberty!

'On those who first should violate   340
Such sacred heralds in their state
Rest the blood that must ensue . . .
And it will not rest on you.

'And if then the tyrants dare,
Let them ride among you there,   345
Slash and stab and maim and hew –
What they like, that let them do.

'With folded arms, and steady eyes,
And little fear, and less surprise,
Look upon them as they slay   350
Till their rage has died away.

'Then they will return with shame
To the place from which they came,
And the blood thus shed will speak
In hot blushes on their cheek: 355

'Every Woman in the land
Will point at them as they stand . . .
They will hardly dare to greet
Their acquaintance in the street.

'And the bold, true warriors   360
Who have hugged Danger in wars
Will turn to those who would be free,
Ashamed of such base company.

'And that slaughter, to the Nation
Shall steam up like inspiration,   365

Eloquent, oracular;
A volcano heard afar.

'And these words shall then become
Like oppression's thundered doom
Ringing through each heart and brain,   370
Heard again, again, again –

' "Rise like lions after slumber
In unvanquishable number,
Shake your chains to earth like dew
Which in sleep had fallen on you –   375
Ye are many – they are few".'

Ode to the West Wind[1]

1

O wild West Wind, thou breath of Autumn's being,
Thou, from whose unseen presence the leaves dead
Are driven, like ghosts from an enchanter fleeing,

Yellow, and black, and pale, and hectic red,
Pestilence-stricken multitudes: O thou,   5
Who chariotest to their dark wintry bed

The wingèd seeds, where they lie cold and low,
Each like a corpse within its grave, until
Thine azure sister of the Spring shall blow

[1] This poem was conceived and chiefly written in a wood that skirts the Arno,
near Florence, and on a day when that tempestuous wind, whose temperature is
at once mild and animating, was collecting the vapours which pour down the
autumnal rains. They began, as I foresaw, at sunset with a violent tempest of hail
and rain, attended by that magnificent thunder and lightning peculiar to the
Cisalpine regions.
   The phenomenon alluded to at the conclusion of the third stanza is well known
to naturalists. The vegetation at the bottom of the sea, of rivers, and of lakes,
sympathises with that of the land in the change of seasons, and is consequently
influenced by the winds which announce it.

Her clarion o'er the dreaming earth, and fill   10
(Driving sweet buds like flocks to feed in air)
With living hues and odours plain and hill:

Wild Spirit, which art moving everywhere;
Destroyer and Preserver; hear, O hear!

2

Thou on whose stream, 'mid the steep sky's commotion,   15
Loose clouds like Earth's decaying leaves are shed,
Shook from the tangled boughs of Heaven and Ocean,

Angels of rain and lightning: there are spread
On the blue surface of thine airy surge,
Like the bright hair uplifted from the head   20

Of some fierce Maenad, even from the dim verge
Of the horizon to the zenith's height,
The locks of the approaching storm. Thou dirge

Of the dying year, to which this closing night
Will be the dome of a vast sepulchre   25
Vaulted with all thy congregated might

Of vapours, from whose solid atmosphere
Black rain, and fire, and hail will burst: O hear!

3

Thou who didst waken from his summer dreams
The blue Mediterranean, where he lay,   30
Lulled by the coil of his crystalline streams,

Beside a pumice isle in Baiae's bay,
And saw in sleep old palaces and towers
Quivering within the wave's intenser day,

All overgrown with azure moss and flowers   35
So sweet, the sense faints picturing them! Thou
For whose path the Atlantic's level powers

Cleave themselves into chasms, while far below
The sea-blooms and the oozy woods which wear
The sapless foliage of the ocean, know   40

Thy voice, and suddenly grow grey with fear,
And tremble and despoil themselves: O hear!

4

If I were a dead leaf thou mightest bear;
If I were a swift cloud to fly with thee;
A wave to pant beneath thy power, and share   45

The impulse of thy strength, only less free
Than thou, O Uncontrollable! If even
I were as in my boyhood, and could be

The comrade of thy wanderings over Heaven,
As then, when to outstrip thy skiey speed   50
Scarce seemed a vision; I would ne'er have striven

As thus with thee in prayer in my sore need.
Oh! lift me as a wave, a leaf, a cloud!
I fall upon the thorns of life! I bleed!

A heavy weight of hours has chained and bowed   55
One too like thee: tameless, and swift, and proud.

5

Make me thy lyre, even as the forest is:
What if my leaves are falling like its own!
The tumult of thy mighty harmonies

Will take from both a deep, autumnal tone   60
Sweet though in sadness. Be thou, Spirit fierce,
My spirit! Be thou me, impetuous one!

Drive my dead thoughts over the universe
Like withered leaves to quicken a new birth!
And, by the incantation of this verse,   65

Scatter, as from an unextinguished hearth
Ashes and sparks, my words among mankind!
Be through my lips to unawakened Earth

The trumpet of a prophecy! O Wind,
If Winter comes, can Spring be far behind?   70

from **Peter Bell The Third**

PART THE THIRD
HELL

Hell is a city much like London –
  A populous and a smoky city;
There are all sorts of people undone,
And there is little or no fun done;
  Small justice shown, and still less pity.   5

There is a Castle, and a Canning,
  A Cobbett, and a Castlereagh;
All sorts of caitiff corpses planning
All sorts of cozening for trepanning
  Corpses less corrupt than they.   10

There is a ***, who has lost
  His wits, or sold them, none knows which;
He walks about a double ghost,
And though as thin as Fraud almost –
  Ever grows more grim and rich.   15

There is a Chancery Court; a King;
  A manufacturing mob; a set
Of thieves who by themselves are sent

Similar thieves to represent;
    An army; and a public debt –   20

Which last is a scheme of Paper money,
    And means – being interpreted –
'Bees, keep your wax – give us the honey,
And we will plant while skies are sunny,
    Flowers, which in winter serve instead.'   25

There is great talk of Revolution –
    And a great chance of Despotism –
German soldiers – camps – confusion –
Tumults – lotteries – rage – delusion –
    Gin – suicide – and methodism.   30

Taxes too, on wine and bread,
    And meat, and beer, and tea, and cheese,
From which those patriots pure are fed
Who gorge before they reel to bed
    The tenfold essence of all these.   35

There are mincing women, mewing
    (Like cats, who *amant miserè*),
Of their own virtue, and pursuing
Their gentler sisters to that ruin,
    Without which – what were chastity?   40

Lawyers – judges – old hobnobbers
    Are there – bailiffs – chancellors –
Bishops – great and little robbers –
Rhymesters – pamphleteers – stock-jobbers –
    Men of glory in the wars, –   45

Things whose trade is, over ladies
    To lean, and flirt, and stare, and simper,
Till all that is divine in woman
Grows cruel, courteous, smooth, inhuman,
    Crucified 'twixt a smile and whimper.   50

Thrusting, toiling, wailing, moiling,
    Frowning, preaching – such a riot!

Each with never-ceasing labour,
Whilst he thinks he cheats his neighbour,
   Cheating his own heart of quiet.   55

And all these meet at levees; –
   Dinners convivial and political; –
Suppers of epic poets; – teas,
Where small talk dies in agonies; –
   Breakfasts professional and critical; –   60

Lunches and snacks so aldermanic
   That one would furnish forth ten dinners,
Where reigns a Cretan-tonguèd panic
Lest news Russ, Dutch, or Alemannic
   Should make some losers, and some winners; – 65

At conversazioni – balls –
   Conventicles – and drawing-rooms –
Courts of law – committees – calls
Of a morning – clubs – book-stalls –
   Churches – masquerades – and tombs.   70

And this is Hell – and in this smother
   All are damnable and damned;
Each one damning, damns the other;
They are damned by one another,
   By none other are they damned.   75

'Tis a lie to say, 'God damns!'
   Where was Heaven's Attorney General
When they first gave out such flams?
Let there be an end of shams,
   They are mines of poisonous mineral.   80

Statesmen damn themselves to be
   Cursed; and lawyers damn their souls
To the auction of a fee;
Churchmen damn themselves to see
   God's sweet love in burning coals.   85

The rich are damned, beyond all cure,
    To taunt, and starve, and trample on
The weak and wretched; and the poor
Damn their broken hearts to endure
    Stripe on stripe, with groan on groan.   90

Sometimes the poor are damned indeed
    To take, – not means for being blest, –
But Cobbett's snuff, revenge; that weed
From which the worms that it doth feed
    Squeeze less than they before possessed.   95

And some few, like we know who,
    Damned – but God alone knows why –
To believe their minds are given
To make this ugly Hell a Heaven;
    In which faith they live and die.   100

Thus, as in a town plague-stricken,
    Each man be he sound or no
Must indifferently sicken;
As when day begins to thicken,
    None knows a pigeon from a crow, –   105

So good and bad, sane and mad,
    The oppressor and the oppressed;
Those who weep to see what others
Smile to inflict upon their brothers;
    Lovers, haters, worst and best;   110

All are damned – they breathe an air
    Thick, infected, joy-dispelling:
Each pursues what seems most fair,
Mining like moles through mind, and there
Scoop palace-caverns vast, where Care   115
    In thronèd state is ever dwelling.

PART THE FOURTH
SIN

Lo, Peter in Hell's Grosvenor-square,
   A footman in the devil's service!
And the misjudging world would swear
That every man in service there   120
   To virtue would prefer vice.

But Peter, though now damned, was not
   What Peter was before damnation.
Men oftentimes prepare a lot
Which, ere it finds them, is not what   125
   Suits with their genuine station.

All things that Peter saw and felt
   Had a peculiar aspect to him;
And when they came within the belt
Of his own nature, seemed to melt,   130
   Like cloud to cloud, into him.

And so, the outward world uniting
   To that within him, he became
Considerably uninviting
To those, who meditation slighting,   135
   Were moulded in a different frame.

And he scorned them, and they scorned him;
   And he scorned all they did; and they
Did all that men of their own trim
Are wont to do to please their whim, –   140
   Drinking, lying, swearing, play.

Such were his fellow-servants; thus
   His virtue, like our own, was built
Too much on that indignant fuss
Hypocrite Pride stirs up in us   145
   To bully one another's guilt.

He had a mind which was somehow
   At once circumference and centre

Of all he might or feel or know;
Nothing went ever out, although 150
   Something did ever enter.

He had as much imagination
   As a pint-pot: – he never could
Fancy another situation,
From which to dart his contemplation, 155
   Than that wherein he stood.

Yet his was individual mind,
   And new created all he saw
In a new manner, and refined
Those new creations, and combined 160
   Them, by a master-spirit's law.

Thus – though unimaginative –
   An apprehension clear, intense,
Of his mind's work, had made alive
The things it wrought on; I believe, 165
   Wakening a sort of thought in sense.

But from the first 'twas Peter's drift
   To be a kind of moral eunuch,
He touched the hem of nature's shift,
Felt faint – and never dared uplift 170
   The closest, all-concealing tunic.

She laughed the while, with an arch smile,
   And kissed him with a sister's kiss,
And said – 'My best Diogenes,
I love you well – but, if you please, 175
   Tempt not again my deepest bliss.

"Tis you are cold – for I, not coy,
   Yield love for love, frank, warm and true;
And Burns, a Scottish peasant boy –
His errors prove it – knew my joy 180
   More, learned friend, than you.

'*Bocca baciata non perde ventura*
   Anzi rinnuova come fa la luna: –
So thought Boccaccio, whose sweet words might cure a
Male prude, like you, from what you now endure, a   185
   Low-tide in soul, like a stagnant laguna.'

Then Peter rubbed his eyes severe,
   And smoothed his spacious forehead down
With his broad palm: – 'twixt love and fear,
He looked, as he no doubt felt, queer;   190
   And in his dream sate down.

The Devil was no uncommon creature;
   A leaden-witted thief – just huddled
Out of the dross and scum of nature;
A toad-like lump of limb and feature,   195
   With mind, and heart, and fancy muddled.

He was that heavy, dull, cold thing
   The spirit of Evil well may be:
A drone too base to have a sting;
Who gluts, and grimes his lazy wing,   200
   And calls lust, luxury.

Now he was quite the kind of wight
   Round whom collect, at a fixed era,
Venison, turtle, hock and claret, –
Good cheer – and those who come to share it –   205
   And best East India madeira!

It was his fancy to invite
   Men of science, wit and learning,
Who came to lend each other light: –
He proudly thought that his gold's might   210
   Had set those spirits burning.

And men of learning, science, wit,
   Considered him as you and I
Think of some rotten tree, and sit
Lounging and dining under it,   215
   Exposed to the wide sky.

And all the while, with loose fat smile
   The willing wretch sat winking there,
Believing 'twas his power that made
That jovial scene – and that all paid   220
   Homage to his unnoticed chair.

Though to be sure this place was Hell;
   He was the Devil – and all they –
What though the claret circled well,
And wit, like ocean, rose and fell? –   225
   Were damned eternally.

England in 1819

An old, mad, blind, despised and dying King;
Princes, the dregs of their dull race, who flow
Through public scorn, – mud from a muddy spring;
Rulers who neither see nor feel nor know,
But leechlike to their fainting Country cling   5
Till they drop, blind in blood, without a blow;
A people starved and stabbed on the untilled field;
An army whom liberticide and prey
Makes as a two-edged sword to all who wield;
Golden and sanguine laws which tempt and slay;   10
Religion Christless, Godless, a book sealed;
A senate, Time's worst statute, unrepealed, –
Are graves from which a glorious Phantom may
Burst, to illumine our tempestuous day.

The Cloud

I bring fresh showers for the thirsting flowers,
    From the seas and the streams;
I bear light shade for the leaves when laid
    In their noon-day dreams.
From my wings are shaken the dews that waken   5
    The sweet buds every one,
When rocked to rest on their mother's breast,
    As she dances about the sun.
I wield the flail of the lashing hail,
    And whiten the green plains under,   10
And then again I dissolve it in rain,
    And laugh as I pass in thunder.

I sift the snow on the mountains below,
    And their great pines groan aghast;
And all the night 'tis my pillow white,   15
    While I sleep in the arms of the blast.
Sublime on the towers of my skiey bowers,
    Lightning my pilot sits,
In a cavern under is fettered the thunder,
    It struggles and howls at fits;   20
Over earth and ocean, with gentle motion,
    This pilot is guiding me,
Lured by the love of the genii that move
    In the depths of the purple sea;
Over the rills, and the crags, and the hills,   25
    Over the lakes and the plains,
Wherever he dream, under mountain or stream,
    The Spirit he loves remains;
And I all the while bask in Heaven's blue smile,
    Whilst he is dissolving in rains.   30

The sanguine sunrise, with his meteor eyes,
    And his burning plumes outspread,
Leaps on the back of my sailing rack,
    When the morning star shines dead;
As on the jag of a mountain crag   35

    Which an earthquake rocks and swings,
An eagle alit one moment may sit
    In the light of its golden wings;
And when sunset may breathe, from the lit sea beneath,
    Its ardours of rest and of love,   40
And the crimson pall of eve may fall
    From the depths of Heaven above,
With wings folded I rest, on mine aery nest,
    As still as a brooding dove.

That orbèd maiden with white fire laden,   45
    Whom mortals call the moon,
Glides glimmering o'er my fleece-like floor,
    By the midnight breezes strewn;
And wherever the beat of her unseen feet,
    Which only the angels hear,   50
May have broken the woof of my tent's thin roof,
    The stars peep behind her, and peer;
And I laugh to see them whirl and flee
    Like a swarm of golden bees,
When I widen the rent in my wind-built tent,   55
    Till the calm rivers, lakes, and seas,
Like strips of the sky fallen through me on high,
    Are each paved with the moon and these.

I bind the sun's throne with a burning zone,
    And the moon's with a girdle of pearl;   60
The volcanoes are dim, and the stars reel and swim,
    When the whirlwinds my banner unfurl.
From cape to cape, with a bridge-like shape,
    Over a torrent sea,
Sunbeam-proof, I hang like a roof –   65
    The mountains its columns be.
The triumphal arch through which I march
    With hurricane, fire, and snow,
When the powers of the air are chained to my chair,
    Is the million-coloured bow;   70
The sphere-fire above its soft colours wove,
    While the moist earth was laughing below.

I am the daughter of Earth and Water,
    And the nursling of the sky;
I pass through the pores of the oceans and shores;   75
    I change, but I cannot die –
For after the rain, when with never a stain
    The pavilion of Heaven is bare,
And the winds and sunbeams, with their convex gleams,
    Build up the blue dome of air,   80
I silently laugh at my own cenotaph,
    And out of the caverns of rain,
Like a child from the womb, like a ghost from the tomb,
    I arise and unbuild it again.

Men of England: A Song

Men of England, wherefore plough
For the lords who lay ye low?
Wherefore weave with toil and care
The rich robes your tyrants wear?

Wherefore feed and clothe and save   5
From the cradle to the grave,
Those ungrateful drones who would
Drain your sweat – nay, drink your blood?

Wherefore, Bees of England, forge
Many a weapon, chain and scourge,   10
That these stingless drones may spoil
The forced produce of your toil?

Have ye leisure, comfort, calm,
Shelter, food, love's gentle balm?
Or what is it ye buy so dear   15
With your pain and with your fear?

The seed ye sow, another reaps;
The wealth ye find, another keeps;

The robes ye weave, another wears;
The arms ye forge, another bears. 20

Sow seed – but let no tyrant reap;
Find wealth – let no impostor heap;
Weave robes – let not the idle wear;
Forge arms – in your defence to bear.

Shrink to your cellars, holes and cells – 25
In halls ye deck another dwells,
Why shake the chains ye wrought, [then] see
The steel ye tempered glance on ye?

With plough and spade and hoe and loom
Trace your grave and build your tomb, 30
And weave your winding-sheet – till fair
England be your sepulchre.

To a Sky-lark

Hail to thee, blithe Spirit!
    Bird thou never wert,
That from Heaven, or near it,
    Pourest thy full heart
In profuse strains of unpremeditated art. 5

Higher still and higher
    From the earth thou springest
Like a cloud of fire;
    The blue deep thou wingest,
And singing still dost soar, and soaring ever singest. 10

In the golden lightning
    Of the sunken Sun,
O'er which clouds are bright'ning,

Thou dost float and run;
Like an unbodied joy whose race is just begun.   15

The pale purple even
    Melts around thy flight;
Like a star of Heaven
    In the broad day-light
Thou art unseen, – but yet I hear thy shrill delight,   20

Keen as are the arrows
    Of that silver sphere
Whose intense lamp narrows
    In the white dawn clear,
Until we hardly see – we feel that it is there.   25

All the earth and air
    With thy voice is loud,
As when night is bare
    From one lonely cloud
The moon rains out her beams, and Heaven is overflowed.   30

What thou art we know not;
    What is most like thee?
From rainbow clouds there flow not
    Drops so bright to see,
As from thy presence showers a rain of melody.   35

Like a Poet hidden
    In the light of thought,
Singing hymns unbidden
    Till the world is wrought
To sympathy with hopes and fears it heeded not: 40

Like a high-born maiden
    In a palace tower,
Soothing her love-laden
    Soul in secret hour
With music sweet as love, which overflows her bower: 45

Like a glow-worm golden
    In a dell of dew,

Scattering unbeholden
   Its aërial hue
Among the flowers and grass which screen it from the view: 50

Like a rose embowered
   In its own green leaves,
By warm winds deflowered,
   Till the scent it gives
Makes faint with too much sweet those heavy-wingèd thieves: 55

Sound of vernal showers
   On the twinkling grass,
Rain-awakened flowers,
   All that ever was
Joyous and clear and fresh, thy music doth surpass.   60

Teach us, Sprite or Bird,
   What sweet thoughts are thine;
I have never heard
   Praise of love or wine
That painted forth a flood of rapture so divine: 65

Chorus Hymenaeal
   Or triumphal chaunt
Matched with thine, would be all
   But an empty vaunt,
A thing wherein we feel there is some hidden want.   70

What objects are the fountains
   Of thy happy strain?
What fields or waves or mountains?
   What shapes of sky or plain?
What love of thine own kind? what ignorance of pain?   75

With thy clear keen joyance
   Languor cannot be –
Shadow of annoyance
   Never came near thee:
Thou lovest – but ne'er knew love's sad satiety.   80

Waking or asleep,
　　Thou of death must deem
Things more true and deep
　　Than we mortals dream
Or how could thy notes flow in such a crystal stream? 　　85

We look before and after
　　And pine for what is not:
Our sincerest laughter
　　With some pain is fraught;
Our sweetest songs are those that tell of saddest thought. 　　90

Yet if we could scorn
　　Hate and pride and fear;
If we were things born
　　Not to shed a tear,
I know not how thy joy we ever should come near. 　　95

Better than all measures
　　Of delightful sound –
Better than all treasures
　　That in books are found –
Thy skill to poet were, thou scorner of the ground! 　　100

Teach me half the gladness
　　That thy brain must know,
Such harmonious madness
　　From my lips would flow,
The world should listen then – as I am listening now. 　　105

from **Letter to Maria Gisborne**

Whoever should behold me now, I wist,
Would think I were a mighty mechanist,
Bent with sublime Archimedean art
To breathe a soul into the iron heart

Of some machine portentous, or strange gin,   5
Which, by the force of figured spells, might win
Its way over the sea, and sport therein;
For round the walls are hung dread engines, such
As Vulcan never wrought for Jove to clutch
Ixion or the Titans; – or the quick   10
Wit of that Man of God, St Dominic,
To convince Atheist, Turk or heretic
Or those in philanthropic council met
Who thought to pay some interest for the debt
They owed to Jesus Christ for their salvation,   15
By giving a faint foretaste of damnation
To Shakespeare, Sidney, Spenser – and the rest
Who made our land an island of the blest,
When lamplike Spain, who now relumes her fire
On Freedom's hearth, grew dim with empire –   20
With thumbscrews, wheels, with tooth and spike and jag,
Which fishers found under the utmost crag
Of Cornwall, and the storm-encompassed isles
Where to the sky the rude sea rarely smiles
Unless in treacherous wrath, as on the morn   25
When the exulting elements, in scorn,
Satiated with destroyed destruction, lay
Sleeping in beauty on their mangled prey,
As Panthers sleep; – and other strange dread
Magical forms the brick floor overspread –   30
Proteus transformed to metal did not make
More figures or more strange, nor did he take
Such shapes of unintelligible brass,
Or heap himself in such a horrid mass
Of tin and iron not to be understood,   35
And forms of unimaginable wood
To puzzle Tubal Cain and all his brood:
Great screws, and cones, and wheels, and groovèd blocks,
The elements of what will stand the shocks
Of wave and wind and time. – Upon the table   40
More knacks and quips there be than I am able
To catalogize in this verse of mine: –
A pretty bowl of wood, not full of wine
But quicksilver, that dew which the gnomes drink

When at their subterranean toil they swink,   45
Pledging the daemons of the earthquake, who
Reply to them in lava, cry halloo!
And call out to the cities o'er their head –
Roofs, towers, and shrines, the dying and the dead,
Crash through the chinks of earth – and then all quaff   50
Another rouse, and hold their ribs and laugh.
This quicksilver no gnome has drunk – within
The walnut bowl it lies, veinèd and thin,
In colour like the wake of light that stains
The Tuscan deep, when from the moist moon rains   55
The inmost shower of its white fire – the breeze
Is still – blue Heaven smiles over the pale Seas.
And in this bowl of quicksilver – for I
Yield to the impulse of an infancy
Outlasting manhood – I have made to float   60
A rude idealism of a paper boat:
A hollow screw with cogs – Henry will know
The thing I mean, and laugh at me, if so
He fears not I should do more mischief – next
Lie bills and calculations much perplexed,   65
With steam boats, frigates and machinery quaint
Traced over them in blue and yellow paint.
Then comes a range of mathematical
Instruments, for plans nautical and statical;
A heap of rosin, a queer broken glass   70
With ink in it, a china cup that was
What it will never be again, I think,
A thing from which sweet lips were wont to drink
The liquor doctors rail at – and which I
Will quaff in spite of them – and when we die   75
We'll toss up who died first of drinking tea,
And cry out, 'Heads or tails?' where'er we be.
Near that a dusty paint box, some odd hooks,
A half-burnt match, an ivory block, three books
Where conic sections, spherics, logarithms,   80
To great Laplace from Saunderson and Sims
Lie heaped in their harmonious disarray
Of figures – disentangle them who may.
Baron de Tott's memoirs beside them lie,

And some odd volumes of old chemistry.   85
Near those a most inexplicable tin thing
With lead in the middle – I'm conjecturing
How to make Henry understand – but, no –
I'll leave, as Spenser says, with many mo,
This secret in the pregnant womb of time,   90
Too vast a matter for so weak a rhyme.

And here like some weird Archimage sit I,
Plotting dark spells and devilish enginery,
The self-impelling steam wheels of the mind
Which pump up oaths from clergymen, and grind   95
The gentle spirit of our meek reviews
Into a powdery foam of salt abuse –
Ruffling the dull wave of their self-content.
I sit, and smile or sigh, as is my bent,
But not for them – Libeccio rushes round   100
With an inconstant and an idle sound,
I heed him more than them – the thundersmoke
Is gathering on the mountains, like a cloak
Folded athwart their shoulders broad and bare;
The ripe corn under the undulating air   105
Undulates like an ocean, – and the vines
Are trembling wide in all their trellised lines –
The murmur of the awakening sea doth fill
The empty pauses of the blast – the hill
Looks hoary through the white electric rain –   110
And from the glens beyond, in sullen strain
The interrupted thunder howls – above
One chasm of Heaven smiles, like the eye of Love,
On the unquiet world – while such things are,
How could one worth your friendship heed this war   115
Of worms? the shriek of the world's carrion jays,
Their censure, or their wonder, or their praise?

from **The Witch of Atlas**

And where within the surface of the river
   The shadows of the massy temples lie,
And never are erased – but tremble ever
   Like things which every cloud can doom to die,
Through lotus-paven canals, and wheresoever   5
   The works of man pierced that serenest sky
With tombs, and towers, and fanes, 'twas her delight
To wander in the shadow of the night.

With motion like the spirit of that wind
   Whose soft step deepens slumber, her light feet   10
Passed through the peopled haunts of humankind,
   Scattering sweet visions from her presence sweet,
Through fane, and palace-court, and labyrinth mined
   With many a dark and subterranean street
Under the Nile, through chambers high and deep   15
She passed, observing mortals in their sleep.

A pleasure sweet doubtless it was to see
   Mortals subdued in all the shapes of sleep.
Here lay two sister twins in infancy;
   There, a lone youth who in his dreams did weep;   20
Within, two lovers linkèd innocently
   In their loose locks which over both did creep
Like ivy from one stem; – and there lay calm
Old age with snow-bright hair and folded palm.

But other troubled forms of sleep she saw,   25
   Not to be mirrored in a holy song –
Distortions foul of supernatural awe,
   And pale imaginings of visioned wrong;
And all the code of Custom's lawless law
   Written upon the brows of old and young: 30
'This,' said the wizard maiden, 'is the strife
Which stirs the liquid surface of man's life.'

And little did the sight disturb her soul. –
   We, the weak mariners of that wide lake

Where'er its shores extend or billows roll,   35
   Our course unpiloted and starless make
O'er its wild surface to an unknown goal: –
   But she in the calm depths her way could take,
Where in bright bowers immortal forms abide
Beneath the weltering of the restless tide.   40

And she saw princes couched under the glow
   Of sunlike gems; and round each temple-court
In dormitories ranged, row after row,
   She saw the priests asleep – all of one sort –
For all were educated to be so. –   45
   The peasants in their huts, and in the port
The sailors she saw cradled on the waves,
And the dead lulled within their dreamless graves.

And all the forms in which those spirits lay
   Were to her sight like the diaphanous   50
Veils, in which those sweet ladies oft array
   Their delicate limbs, who would conceal from us
Only their scorn of all concealment: they
   Move in the light of their own beauty thus.
But these and all now lay with sleep upon them,   55
And little thought a Witch was looking on them.

She, all those human figures breathing there
   Beheld as living spirits – to her eyes
The naked beauty of the soul lay bare,
   And often through a rude and worn disguise   60
She saw the inner form most bright and fair –
   And then she had a charm of strange device,
Which, murmured on mute lips with tender tone,
Could make that spirit mingle with her own.

Alas! Aurora, what wouldst thou have given   65
   For such a charm when Tithon became gray?
Or how much, Venus, of thy silver heaven
   Wouldst thou have yielded, ere Proserpina
Had half (oh! why not all?) the debt forgiven

Which dear Adonis had been doomed to pay,   70
To any witch who would have taught you it?
The Heliad doth not know its value yet.

'Tis said in after times her spirit free
    Knew what love was, and felt itself alone –
But holy Dian could not chaster be   75
    Before she stooped to kiss Endymion,
Than now this lady – like a sexless bee
    Tasting all blossoms, and confined to none,
Among those mortal forms, the wizard-maiden
Passed with an eye serene and heart unladen.   80

To those she saw most beautiful, she gave
    Strange panacea in a crystal bowl: –
They drank in their deep sleep of that sweet wave,
    And lived thenceforward as if some control,
Mightier than life, were in them; and the grave   85
    Of such, when death oppressed the weary soul,
Was as a green and overarching bower
Lit by the gems of many a starry flower.

For on the night that they were buried, she
    Restored the embalmers' ruining, and shook   90
The light out of the funeral lamps, to be
    A mimic day within that deathy nook;
And she unwound the woven imagery
    Of second childhood's swaddling bands, and took
The coffin, its last cradle, from its niche,   95
And threw it with contempt into a ditch.

And there the body lay, age after age,
    Mute, breathing, beating, warm, and undecaying,
Like one asleep in a green hermitage,
    With gentle smiles about its eyelids playing,   100
And living in its dreams beyond the rage
    Of death or life; while they were still arraying
In liveries ever new, the rapid, blind
And fleeting generations of mankind.

And she would write strange dreams upon the brain 105
   Of those who were less beautiful, and make
All harsh and crooked purposes more vain
   Than in the desert is the serpent's wake
Which the sand covers – all his evil gain
   The miser in such dreams would rise and shake 110
Into a beggar's lap; – the lying scribe
Would his own lies betray without a bribe.

The priests would write an explanation full,
   Translating hieroglyphics into Greek,
How the God Apis really was a bull, 115
   And nothing more; and bid the herald stick
The same against the temple doors, and pull
   The old cant down; they licensed all to speak
Whate'er they thought of hawks, and cats, and geese,
By pastoral letters to each diocese. 120

The king would dress an ape up in his crown
   And robes, and seat him on his glorious seat,
And on the right hand of the sunlike throne
   Would place a gaudy mock-bird to repeat
The chatterings of the monkey. – Every one 125
   Of the prone courtiers crawled to kiss the feet
Of their great Emperor, when the morning came,
And kissed – alas, how many kiss the same!

The soldiers dreamed that they were blacksmiths, and
   Walked out of quarters in somnambulism; 130
Round the red anvils you might see them stand
   Like Cyclopses in Vulcan's sooty abysm,
Beating their swords to ploughshares; – in a band
   The gaolers sent those of the liberal schism
Free through the streets of Mephis, much, I wis, 135
To the annoyance of king Amasis.

And timid lovers who had been so coy,
   They hardly knew whether they loved or not,
Would rise out of their rest, and take sweet joy,
   To the fulfilment of their inmost thought; 140

And when next day the maiden and the boy
   Met one another, both, like sinners caught,
Blushed at the thing which each believed was done
Only in fancy – till the tenth moon shone;

And then the Witch would let them take no ill: 145
   Of many thousand schemes which lovers find,
The Witch found one, – and so they took their fill
   Of happiness in marriage warm and kind.
Friends who, by practice of some envious skill,
   Were torn apart – a wide wound, mind from mind! –   150
She did unite again with visions clear
Of deep affection and of truth sincere.

These were the pranks she played among the cities
   Of mortal men, and what she did to Sprites
And Gods, entangling them in her sweet ditties   155
   To do her will, and show their subtle sleights,
I will declare another time; for it is
   A tale more fit for the weird winter nights
Than for these garish summer days, when we
Scarcely believe much more than we can see.   160

To the Moon

    Art thou pale for weariness
Of climbing Heaven, and gazing on the earth,
    Wandering companionless
Among the stars that have a different birth, –
And ever changing, like a joyless eye   5
That finds no object worth its constancy?

from **Epipsychidion: Verses Addressed to the Noble and Unfortunate Lady, Emilia V—, Now Imprisoned in the Convent of —**

She met me, Stranger, upon life's rough way,
And lured me towards sweet Death; as Night by Day,
Winter by Spring, or Sorrow by swift Hope,
Led into light, life, peace. An antelope,
In the suspended impulse of its lightness,   5
Were less ethereally light: the brightness
Of her divinest presence trembles through
Her limbs, as underneath a cloud of dew
Embodied in the windless Heaven of June
Amid the splendour-wingèd stars, the Moon   10
Burns, inextinguishably beautiful:
And from her lips, as from a hyacinth full
Of honey-dew, a liquid murmur drops,
Killing the sense with passion; sweet as stops
Of planetary music heard in trance.   15
In her mild lights the starry spirits dance,
The sun-beams of those wells which ever leap
Under the lightnings of the soul – too deep
For the brief fathom-line of thought or sense.
The glory of her being, issuing thence,   20
Stains the dead, blank, cold air with a warm shade
Of unentangled intermixture, made
By Love, of light and motion: one intense
Diffusion, one serene Omnipresence,
Whose flowing outlines mingle in their flowing,   25
Around her cheeks and utmost fingers glowing
With the unintermitted blood, which there
Quivers, (as in a fleece of snow-like air
The crimson pulse of living morning quiver,)
Continuously prolonged, and ending never,   30
Till they are lost, and in that Beauty furled
Which penetrates and clasps and fills the world;
Scarce visible from extreme loveliness.
Warm fragrance seems to fall from her light dress,

And her loose hair; and where some heavy tress   35
The air of her own speed has disentwined,
The sweetness seems to satiate the faint wind;
And in the soul a wild odour is felt,
Beyond the sense, like fiery dews that melt
Into the bosom of a frozen bud. –   40
See where she stands! a mortal shape indued
With love and life and light and deity,
And motion which may change but cannot die;
An image of some bright Eternity;
A shadow of some golden dream; a Splendour   45
Leaving the third sphere pilotless; a tender
Reflection of the eternal Moon of Love
Under whose motions life's dull billows move;
A Metaphor of Spring and Youth and Morning;
A Vision like incarnate April, warning,   50
With smiles and tears, Frost the Anatomy
Into his summer grave.

Ah, woe is me!
What have I dared? where am I lifted? how
Shall I descend, and perish not? I know
That Love makes all things equal: I have heard   55
By mine own heart this joyous truth averred:
The spirit of the worm beneath the sod
In love and worship, blends itself with God.

Spouse! Sister! Angel! Pilot of the Fate
Whose course has been so starless! O too late   60
Belovèd! O too soon adored, by me!
For in the fields of immortality
My spirit should at first have worshipped thine,
A divine presence in a place divine;
Or should have moved beside it on this earth,   65
A shadow of that substance, from its birth;
But not as now: – I love thee; yes, I feel
That on the fountain of my heart a seal
Is set, to keep its waters pure and bright
For thee, since in those *tears* thou hast delight.   70
We – are we not formed, as notes of music are,

For one another, though dissimilar;
Such difference without discord, as can make
Those sweetest sounds in which all spirits shake
As trembling leaves in a continuous air? 75

Thy wisdom speaks in me, and bids me dare
Beacon the rocks on which high hearts are wrecked.
I never was attached to that great sect
Whose doctrine is, that each one should select
Out of the crowd a mistress or a friend, 80
And all the rest, though fair and wise, commend
To cold oblivion, though it is in the code
Of modern morals, and the beaten road
Which those poor slaves with weary footsteps tread,
Who travel to their home among the dead 85
By the broad highway of the world, and so
With one chained friend, perhaps a jealous foe,
The dreariest and the longest journey go.

True Love in this differs from gold and clay,
That to divide is not to take away. 90
Love is like understanding, that grows bright,
Gazing on many truths; 'tis like thy light,
Imagination! which from earth and sky,
And from the depths of human fantasy,
As from a thousand prisms and mirrors, fills 95
The Universe with glorious beams, and kills
Error, the worm, with many a sun-like arrow
Of its reverberated lightning. Narrow
The heart that loves, the brain that contemplates,
The life that wears, the spirit that creates 100
One object, and one form, and builds thereby
A sepulchre for its eternity.

Mind from its object differs most in this:
Evil from good; misery from happiness;
The baser from the nobler; the impure 105
And frail, from what is clear and must endure.
If you divide suffering and dross, you may
Diminish till it is consumed away;

If you divide pleasure and love and thought,
Each part exceeds the whole; and we know not   110
How much, while any yet remains unshared,
Of pleasure may be gained, of sorrow spared:
This truth is that deep well, whence sages draw
The unenvied light of hope; the eternal law
By which those live, to whom this world of life   115
Is as a garden ravaged, and whose strife
Tills for the promise of a later birth
The wilderness of this Elysian earth.

Adonais: An Elegy on the Death of John Keats, Author of Endymion, Hyperion, etc.

1

I weep for Adonais – he is dead!
O, weep for Adonais! though our tears
Thaw not the frost which binds so dear a head!
And thou, sad Hour, selected from all years
To mourn our loss, rouse thy obscure compeers,   5
And teach them thine own sorrow, say: with me
Died Adonais; till the Future dares
Forget the Past, his fate and fame shall be
An echo and a light unto eternity!

2

Where wert thou, mighty Mother, when he lay,   10
When thy Son lay, pierced by the shaft which flies
In darkness? where was lorn Urania
When Adonais died? With veilèd eyes,
Mid listening Echoes, in her Paradise
She sate, while one, with soft enamoured breath,   15
Rekindled all the fading melodies
With which, like flowers that mock the corse beneath,
He had adorned and hid the coming bulk of death.

3

O, weep for Adonais – he is dead!
Wake, melancholy Mother, wake and weep! 20
Yet wherefore? Quench within their burning bed
Thy fiery tears, and let thy loud heart keep
Like his, a mute and uncomplaining sleep;
For he is gone, where all things wise and fair
Descend; – oh, dream not that the amorous Deep 25
Will yet restore him to the vital air;
Death feeds on his mute voice, and laughs at our despair.

4

Most musical of mourners, weep again!
Lament anew, Urania! – He died,
Who was the Sire of an immortal strain, 30
Blind, old, and lonely, when his country's pride
The priest, the slave, and the liberticide
Trampled and mocked with many a loathèd rite
Of lust and blood; he went, unterrified,
Into the gulf of death; but his clear Sprite 35
Yet reigns o'er earth; the third among the sons of light.

5

Most musical of mourners, weep anew!
Not all to that bright station dared to climb;
And happier they their happiness who knew,
Whose tapers yet burn through that night of time 40
In which suns perished; others more sublime,
Struck by the envious wrath of man or God,
Have sunk, extinct in their refulgent prime;
And some yet live, treading the thorny road
Which leads, through toil and hate, to Fame's serene abode. 45

6

But now, thy youngest, dearest one, has perished –
The nursling of thy widowhood, who grew,
Like a pale flower by some sad maiden cherished,
And fed with true love tears, instead of dew;
Most musical of mourners, weep anew! 50

Thy extreme hope, the loveliest and the last,
The bloom, whose petals nipped before they blew
Died on the promise of the fruit, is waste;
The broken lily lies – the storm is overpast.

7

To that high Capital, where kingly Death   55
Keeps his pale court in beauty and decay,
He came; and bought, with price of purest breath,
A grave among the eternal. – Come away!
Haste, while the vault of blue Italian day
Is yet his fitting charnel-roof! while still   60
He lies, as if in dewy sleep he lay;
Awake him not! surely he takes his fill
Of deep and liquid rest, forgetful of all ill.

8

He will awake no more, oh, never more! –
Within the twilight chamber spreads apace   65
The shadow of white Death, and at the door
Invisible Corruption waits to trace
His extreme way to her dim dwelling-place;
The eternal Hunger sits, but pity and awe
Soothe her pale rage, nor dares she to deface   70
So fair a prey, till darkness, and the law
Of change, shall o'er his sleep the mortal curtain draw.

9

O, weep for Adonais! – The quick Dreams,
The passion-wingèd Ministers of thought,
Who were his flocks, whom near the living streams   75
Of his young spirit he fed, and whom he taught
The love which was its music, wander not, –
Wander no more, from kindling brain to brain,
But droop there, whence they sprung; and mourn their lot
Round the cold heart, where, after their sweet pain   80
They ne'er will gather strength, or find a home again.

10

And one with trembling hands clasps his cold head,
And fans him with her moonlight wings, and cries,

'Our love, our hope, our sorrow, is not dead;
See, on the silken fringe of his faint eyes,   85
Like dew upon a sleeping flower, there lies
A tear some Dream has loosened from his brain.'
Lost Angel of a ruined Paradise!
She knew not 'twas her own; as with no stain
She faded, like a cloud which had outwept its rain.   90

11

One from a lucid urn of starry dew
Washed his light limbs as if embalming them;
Another clipped her profuse locks, and threw
The wreath upon him, like an anadem,
Which frozen tears instead of pearls begem;   95
Another in her wilful grief would break
Her bow and wingèd reeds, as if to stem
A greater loss with one which was more weak;
And dull the barbèd fire against his frozen cheek.

12

Another Splendour on his mouth alit,   100
That mouth, whence it was wont to draw the breath
Which gave it strength to pierce the guarded wit,
And pass into the panting heart beneath
With lightning and with music: the damp death
Quenched its caress upon his icy lips;   105
And, as a dying meteor stains a wreath
Of moonlight vapour, which the cold night clips,
It flushed through his pale limbs, and passed to its eclipse.

13

And others came . . . Desires and Adorations,
Wingèd Persuasions and veiled Destinies,   110
Splendours, and Glooms, and glimmering Incarnations
Of hopes and fears, and twilight Fantasies;
And Sorrow, with her family of Sighs,
And Pleasure, blind with tears, led by the gleam
Of her own dying smile instead of eyes,   115
Came in slow pomp; – the moving pomp might seem
Like pageantry of mist on an autumnal stream.

14

All he had loved, and moulded into thought,
From shape, and hue, and odour, and sweet sound,
Lamented Adonais. Morning sought   120
Her eastern watch-tower, and her hair unbound,
Wet with the tears which should adorn the ground,
Dimmed the aërial eyes that kindle day;
Afar the melancholy thunder moaned,
Pale Ocean in unquiet slumber lay,   125
And the wild winds flew round, sobbing in their dismay.

15

Lost Echo sits amid the voiceless mountains,
And feeds her grief with his remembered lay,
And will no more reply to winds or fountains,
Or amorous birds perched on the young green spray,   130
Or herdsman's horn, or bell at closing day,
Since she can mimic not his lips, more dear
Than those for whose disdain she pined away
Into a shadow of all sounds: – a drear
Murmur, between their songs, is all the woodmen hear.   135

16

Grief made the young Spring wild, and she threw down
Her kindling buds, as if she Autumn were,
Or they dead leaves; since her delight is flown,
For whom should she have waked the sullen year?
To Phoebus was not Hyacinth so dear   140
Nor to himself Narcissus, as to both
Thou, Adonais: wan they stand and sere
Amid the faint companions of their youth,
With dew all turned to tears; odour, to sighing ruth.

17

Thy spirit's sister, the lorn nightingale   145
Mourns not her mate with such melodious pain;
Not so the eagle, who like thee could scale
Heaven, and could nourish in the sun's domain
Her mighty youth with morning, doth complain,
Soaring and screaming round her empty nest,   150

As Albion wails for thee: the curse of Cain
Light on his head who pierced thy innocent breast,
And scared the angel soul that was its earthly guest!

18

Ah, woe is me! Winter is come and gone,
But grief returns with the revolving year;   155
The airs and streams renew their joyous tone;
The ants, the bees, the swallows reappear;
Fresh leaves and flowers deck the dead Season's bier;
The amorous birds now pair in every brake,
And build their mossy homes in field and brere;   160
And the green lizard, and the golden snake,
Like unimprisoned flames, out of their trance awake.

19

Through wood and stream and field and hill and Ocean
A quickening life from the Earth's heart has burst
As it has ever done, with change and motion,   165
From the great morning of the world when first
God dawned on Chaos; in its stream immersed,
The lamps of Heaven flash with a softer light;
All baser things pant with life's sacred thirst;
Diffuse themselves; and spend in love's delight   170
The beauty and the joy of their renewèd might.

20

The leprous corpse touched by this spirit tender
Exhales itself in flowers of gentle breath;
Like incarnations of the stars, when splendour
Is changed to fragrance, they illumine death   175
And mock the merry worm that wakes beneath;
Nought we know, dies. Shall that alone which knows
Be as a sword consumed before the sheath
By sightless lightning? – the intense atom glows
A moment, then is quenched in a most cold repose.   180

21

Alas! that all we loved of him should be,
But for our grief, as if it had not been,

And grief itself be mortal! Woe is me!
Whence are we, and why are we? of what scene
The actors or spectators? Great and mean   185
Meet massed in death, who lends what life must borrow.
As long as skies are blue, and fields are green,
Evening must usher night, night urge the morrow,
Month follow month with woe, and year wake year to sorrow.

22

He will awake no more, oh, never more!   190
'Wake thou,' cried Misery, 'childless Mother, rise
Out of thy sleep, and slake, in thy heart's core,
A wound more fierce than his with tears and sighs.'
And all the Dreams that watched Urania's eyes,
And all the Echoes whom their sister's song
Had held in holy silence, cried: 'Arise!'
Swift as a Thought by the snake Memory stung,
From her ambrosial rest the fading Splendour sprung.

23

She rose like an autumnal Night, that springs
Out of the East, and follows wild and drear   200
The golden Day, which, on eternal wings,
Even as a ghost abandoning a bier,
Has left the Earth a corpse. Sorrow and fear
So struck, so roused, so rapt Urania;
So saddened round her like an atmosphere   205
Of stormy mist; so swept her on her way
Even to the mournful place where Adonais lay.

24

Out of her secret Paradise she sped,
Through camps and cities rough with stone, and steel,
And human hearts, which to her aery tread   210
Yielding not, wounded the invisible
Palms of her tender feet where'er they fell:
And barbèd tongues, and thoughts more sharp than they,
Rent the soft Form they never could repel,
Whose sacred blood, like the young tears of May,   215
Paved with eternal flowers that undeserving way.

25

In the death-chamber for a moment Death,
Shamed by the presence of that living Might,
Blushed to annihilation, and the breath
Revisited those lips, and life's pale light   220
Flashed through those limbs, so late her dear delight.
'Leave me not wild and drear and comfortless,
As silent lightning leaves the starless night!
Leave me not!' cried Urania: her distress
Roused Death: Death rose and smiled, and met her vain caress.

26

'Stay yet awhile! speak to me once again;
Kiss me, so long but as a kiss may live;
And in my heartless breast and burning brain
That word, that kiss, shall all thoughts else survive,
With food of saddest memory kept alive,   230
Now thou art dead, as if it were a part
Of thee, my Adonais! I would give
All that I am to be as thou now art!
But I am chained to Time, and cannot thence depart!

27

'Oh gentle child, beautiful as thou wert,   235
Why didst thou leave the trodden paths of men
Too soon, and with weak hands though mighty heart
Dare the unpastured dragon in his den?
Defenceless as thou wert, oh where was then
Wisdom the mirrored shield, or scorn the spear?   240
Or hadst thou waited the full cycle, when
Thy spirit should have filled its crescent sphere,
The monsters of life's waste had fled from thee like deer.

28

'The herded wolves, bold only to pursue;
The obscene ravens, clamorous o'er the dead;   245
The vultures to the conqueror's banner true
Who feed where Desolation first has fed,
And whose wings rain contagion; – how they fled,

When like Apollo, from his golden bow,
The Pythian of the age one arrow sped   250
And smiled! – The spoilers tempt no second blow,
They fawn on the proud feet that spurn them lying low.

29

'The sun comes forth, and many reptiles spawn;
He sets, and each ephemeral insect then
Is gathered into death without a dawn,   255
And the immortal stars awake again;
So is it in the world of living men:
A godlike mind soars forth, in its delight
Making earth bare and veiling heaven, and when
It sinks, the swarms that dimmed or shared its light   260
Leave to its kindred lamps the spirit's awful night.'

30

Thus ceased she: and the mountain shepherds came,
Their garlands sere, their magic mantles rent;
The Pilgrim of Eternity, whose fame
Over his living head like Heaven is bent,   265
An early but enduring monument,
Came, veiling all the lightnings of his song
In sorrow; from her wilds Ierne sent
The sweetest lyrist of her saddest wrong,
And love taught grief to fall like music from his tongue.   270

31

Midst others of less note, came one frail Form,
A phantom among men; companionless
As the last cloud of an expiring storm
Whose thunder is its knell; he, as I guess,
Had gazed on Nature's naked loveliness,   275
Actaeon-like, and now he fled astray
With feeble steps o'er the world's wilderness,
And his own thoughts, along that rugged way,
Pursued, like raging hounds, their father and their prey.

32

A pardlike Spirit beautiful and swift –   280
A Love in desolation masked; – a Power
Girt round with weakness; – it can scarce uplift
The weight of the superincumbent hour;
It is a dying lamp, a falling shower,
A breaking billow; – even whilst we speak   285
Is it not broken? On the withering flower
The killing sun smiles brightly: on a cheek
The life can burn in blood, even while the heart may break.

33

His head was bound with pansies overblown,
And faded violets, white, and pied, and blue;   290
And a light spear topped with a cypress cone,
Round whose rude shaft dark ivy tresses grew
Yet dripping with the forest's noonday dew,
Vibrated, as the ever-beating heart
Shook the weak hand that grasped it; of that crew   295
He came the last, neglected and apart;
A herd-abandoned deer struck by the hunter's dart.

34

All stood aloof, and at his partial moan
Smiled through their tears; well knew that gentle band
Who in another's fate now wept his own –   300
As in the accents of an unknown land
He sung new sorrow; sad Urania scanned
The Stranger's mien, and murmured: 'Who art thou?'
He answered not, but with a sudden hand
Made bare his branded and ensanguined brow,   305
Which was like Cain's or Christ's – Oh! that it should be so!

35

What softer voice is hushed over the dead?
Athwart what brow is that dark mantle thrown?
What form leans sadly o'er the white death-bed,
In mockery of monumental stone,   310
The heavy heart heaving without a moan?
If it be He, who gentlest of the wise,

Taught, soothed, loved, honoured the departed one,
Let me not vex, with inharmonious sighs,
The silence of that heart's accepted sacrifice.   315

36

Our Adonais has drunk poison – oh!
What deaf and viperous murderer could crown
Life's early cup with such a draught of woe?
The nameless worm would now itself disown:
It felt, yet could escape, the magic tone   320
Whose prelude held all envy, hate, and wrong,
But what was howling in one breast alone,
Silent with expectation of the song,
Whose master's hand is cold, whose silver lyre unstrung.

37

Live thou, whose infamy is not thy fame!   325
Live! fear no heavier chastisement from me,
Thou noteless blot on a remembered name!
But be thyself, and know thyself to be!
And ever at thy season be thou free
To spill the venom when thy fangs o'erflow: 330
Remorse and Self-contempt shall cling to thee;
Hot Shame shall burn upon thy secret brow,
And like a beaten hound tremble thou shalt – as now.

38

Nor let us weep that our delight is fled
Far from these carrion kites that scream below;   335
He wakes or sleeps with the enduring dead;
Thou canst not soar where he is sitting now. –
Dust to the dust! but the pure spirit shall flow
Back to the burning fountain whence it came,
A portion of the Eternal, which must glow   340
Through time and change, unquenchably the same,
Whilst thy cold embers choke the sordid hearth of shame.

39

Peace, peace! he is not dead, he doth not sleep –
He hath awakened from the dream of life –

'Tis we, who lost in stormy visions, keep   345
With phantoms an unprofitable strife,
And in mad trance, strike with our spirit's knife
Invulnerable nothings. – *We* decay
Like corpses in a charnel; fear and grief
Convulse us and consume us day by day,   350
And cold hopes swarm like worms within our living clay.

40

He has outsoared the shadow of our night;
Envy and calumny and hate and pain,
And that unrest which men miscall delight,
Can touch him not and torture not again;   355
From the contagion of the world's slow stain
He is secure, and now can never mourn
A heart grown cold, a head grown grey in vain;
Nor, when the spirit's self has ceased to burn,
With sparkless ashes load an unlamented urn.   360

41

He lives, he wakes – 'tis Death is dead, not he;
Mourn not for Adonais. – Thou young Dawn
Turn all thy dew to splendour, for from thee
The spirit thou lamentest is not gone;
Ye caverns and ye forests, cease to moan!   365
Cease ye faint flowers and fountains, and thou Air
Which like a mourning veil thy scarf hadst thrown
O'er the abandoned Earth, now leave it bare
Even to the joyous stars which smile on its despair!

42

He is made one with Nature: there is heard   370
His voice in all her music, from the moan
Of thunder, to the song of night's sweet bird;
He is a presence to be felt and known
In darkness and in light, from herb and stone,
Spreading itself where'er that Power may move   375
Which has withdrawn his being to its own;
Which wields the world with never wearied love,
Sustains it from beneath, and kindles it above.

43

He is a portion of the loveliness
Which once he made more lovely: he doth bear   380
His part, while the one Spirit's plastic stress
Sweeps through the dull dense world, compelling there
All new successions to the forms they wear;
Torturing th'unwilling dross that checks its flight
To its own likeness, as each mass may bear;   385
And bursting in its beauty and its might
From trees and beasts and men into the Heaven's light.

44

The splendours of the firmament of time
May be eclipsed, but are extinguished not;
Like stars to their appointed height they climb,   390
And death is a low mist which cannot blot
The brightness it may veil. When lofty thought
Lifts a young heart above its mortal lair,
And love and life contend in it, for what
Shall be its earthly doom, the dead live there   395
And move like winds of light on dark and stormy air.

45

The inheritors of unfulfilled renown
Rose from their thrones, built beyond mortal thought,
Far in the Unapparent. Chatterton
Rose pale, his solemn agony had not   400
Yet faded from him; Sidney as he fought
And as he fell and as he lived and loved
Sublimely mild, a Spirit without spot,
Arose; and Lucan, by his death approved:
Oblivion as they rose shrank like a thing reproved.   405

46

And many more, whose names on Earth are dark,
But whose transmitted effluence cannot die
So long as fire outlives the parent spark,
Rose, robed in dazzling immortality.
'Thou art become as one of us,' they cry,   410
'It was for thee yon kingless sphere has long

Swung blind in unascended majesty,
Silent alone amid an Heaven of Song.
Assume thy wingèd throne, thou Vesper of our throng!'

47

Who mourns for Adonais? oh, come forth   415
Fond wretch! and know thyself and him aright,
Clasp with thy panting soul the pendulous Earth;
As from a centre, dart thy spirit's light
Beyond all worlds, until its spacious might
Satiate the void circumference: then shrink   420
Even to a point within our day and night;
And keep thy heart light lest it make thee sink
When hope has kindled hope, and lured thee to the brink;

48

Or go to Rome, which is the sepulchre,
O, not of him, but of our joy: 'tis nought   425
That ages, empires, and religions there
Lie buried in the ravage they have wrought;
For such as he can lend, – they borrow not
Glory from those who made the world their prey;
And he is gathered to the kings of thought   430
Who waged contention with their time's decay,
And of the past are all that cannot pass away.

49

Go thou to Rome, – at once the Paradise,
The grave, the city, and the wilderness;
And where its wrecks like shattered mountains rise,   435
And flowering weeds, and fragrant copses dress
The bones of Desolation's nakedness
Pass, till the Spirit of the spot shall lead
Thy footsteps to a slope of green access
Where, like an infant's smile, over the dead,   440
A light of laughing flowers along the grass is spread.

50

And grey walls moulder round, on which dull Time
Feeds, like slow fire upon a hoary brand:

And one keen pyramid with wedge sublime,
Pavilioning the dust of him who planned   445
This refuge for his memory, doth stand
Like flame transformed to marble; and beneath,
A field is spread, on which a newer band
Have pitched in Heaven's smile their camp of death,
Welcoming him we lose with scarce extinguished breath.   450

51

Here pause: these graves are all too young as yet
To have outgrown the sorrow which consigned
Its charge to each; and if the seal is set,
Here, on one fountain of a mourning mind,
Break it not thou! too surely shalt thou find   455
Thine own well full, if thou returnest home,
Of tears and gall. From the world's bitter wind
Seek shelter in the shadow of the tomb.
What Adonais is, why fear we to become?

52

The One remains, the many change and pass;   460
Heaven's light forever shines, Earth's shadows fly;
Life, like a dome of many-coloured glass,
Stains the white radiance of Eternity,
Until Death tramples it to fragments. – Die,
If thou wouldst be with that which thou dost seek!   465
Follow where all is fled! – Rome's azure sky,
Flowers, ruins, statues, music, words, are weak
The glory they transfuse with fitting truth to speak.

53

Why linger, why turn back, why shrink, my Heart?
Thy hopes are gone before: from all things here   470
They have departed; thou shouldst now depart!
A light is passed from the revolving year,
And man, and woman; and what still is dear
Attracts to crush, repels to make thee wither.
The soft sky smiles, – the low wind whispers near: 475
'Tis Adonais calls! oh, hasten thither,
No more let Life divide what Death can join together.

54

That Light whose smile kindles the Universe,
That Beauty in which all things work and move,
That Benediction which the eclipsing Curse   480
Of birth can quench not, that sustaining Love
Which through the web of being blindly wove
By man and beast and earth and air and sea,
Burns bright or dim, as each are mirrors of
The fire for which all thirst, now beams on me,   485
Consuming the last clouds of cold mortality.

55

The breath whose might I have invoked in song
Descends on me; my spirit's bark is driven
Far from the shore, far from the trembling throng
Whose sails were never to the tempest given;   490
The massy earth and spherèd skies are riven!
I am borne darkly, fearfully, afar;
Whilst burning through the inmost veil of Heaven,
The soul of Adonais, like a star,
Beacons from the abode where the Eternal are.   495

The Aziola

'Do you not hear the aziola cry?
Methinks she must be nigh –'
    Said Mary as we sate
In dusk, ere stars were lit or candles brought –
    And I who thought   5
This Aziola was some tedious woman
Asked, 'Who is Aziola?' – how elate
I felt to know that it was nothing human,
No mockery of myself to fear or hate!
    And Mary saw my soul,   10

And laughed and said – 'Disquiet yourself not,
    'Tis nothing but a little downy owl.'

Sad aziola, many an eventide
    Thy music I had heard
By wood and stream, meadow and mountainside,   15
And fields and marshes wide,
Such as nor voice, nor lute, nor wind, nor bird
    The soul ever stirred –
Unlike and far sweeter than them all.
Sad aziola, from that moment I   20
Loved thee and thy sad cry.

from Hellas: A Lyrical Drama

The world's great age begins anew,
    The golden years return,
The earth doth like a snake renew
    Her winter weeds outworn;
Heaven smiles, and faiths and empires gleam   5
Like wrecks of a dissolving dream.

A brighter Hellas rears its mountains
    From waves serener far,
A new Peneus rolls his fountains
    Against the morning-star;   10
Where fairer Tempes bloom, there sleep
Young Cyclads on a sunnier deep.

A loftier Argo cleaves the main
    Fraught with a later prize;
Another Orpheus sings again,   15
    And loves, and weeps, and dies;
A new Ulysses leaves once more
Calypso for his native shore.

O, write no more the tale of Troy,
    If earth Death's scroll must be!   20
Nor mix with Laian rage the joy
    Which dawns upon the free;
Although a subtler Sphinx renew
Riddles of death Thebes never knew.

Another Athens shall arise,   25
    And to remoter time
Bequeath, like sunset to the skies,
    The splendour of its prime;
And leave, if nought so bright may live,
All earth can take or Heaven can give.   30

Saturn and Love their long repose
    Shall burst, more bright and good
Than all who fell, than One who rose,
    Than many unsubdued;
Not gold, not blood, their altar dowers,   35
But votive tears and symbol flowers.

O cease! must hate and death return?
    Cease! must men kill and die?
Cease! drain not to its dregs the urn
    Of bitter prophecy.
The world is weary of the past,   40
O might it die or rest at last!

O World, O Life, O Time

O World, O Life, O Time,
    On whose last steps I climb,
Trembling at that where I had stood before –
    When will return the glory of your prime?
        No more, O never more!   5

Out of the day and night
A joy has taken flight –
Fresh spring and summer [   ] and winter hoar
Move my faint heart with grief, but with delight
No more, O never more!   10

One Word Is Too Often Profaned

One word is too often profaned
    For me to profane it,
One feeling too falsely disdained
    For thee to disdain it;
One hope is too like despair   5
    For prudence to smother,
And pity from thee more dear
    Than that from another.

I can give not what men call love;
    But wilt thou accept not   10
The worship the heart lifts above
    And the Heavens reject not, –
The desire of the moth for the star,
    Of the night for the morrow,
The devotion to something afar   15
    From the sphere of our sorrow?

To Jane

The keen stars were twinkling
And the fair moon was rising among them,
    Dear Jane.
The guitar was tinkling

But the notes were not sweet till you sung them   5
    Again. –

    As the moon's soft splendour
O'er the faint cold starlight of Heaven
    Is thrown –
So your voice most tender   10
To the strings without soul had then given
    Its own.

    The stars will awaken,
Though the moon sleep a full hour later,
    Tonight;   15
    No leaf will be shaken
While the dews of your melody scatter
    Delight.

    Though the sound overpowers,
Sing again, with your dear voice revealing   20
    A tone
Of some world far from ours,
Where music and moonlight and feeling
    Are one.

Lines Written in the Bay of Lerici

Bright wanderer, fair coquette of Heaven,
To whom alone it has been given
To change and be adored for ever,
Envy not this dim world, for never
But once within its shadow grew   5
One fair as [thou], but far more true. –
She left me at the silent time
When the moon had ceased to climb
The azure dome of Heaven's steep,

And like an albatross asleep,   10
Balanced on her wings of light,
Hovered in the purple night,
Ere she sought her Ocean nest
In the chambers of the west. –
She left me, and I stayed alone   15
Thinking over every tone,
Which though now silent to the ear
The enchanted heart could hear
Like notes which die when born, but still
Haunt the echoes of the hill: 20
And feeling ever – O too much –
The soft vibrations of her touch,
As if her gentle hand even now
Lightly trembled on my brow;
And thus although she absent were   25
Memory gave me all of her
That even fancy dares to claim. –
Her presence had made weak and tame
All passions, and I lived alone
In the time which is our own;   30
The past and future were forgot
As they had been, and would be, not. –
But soon, the guardian angel gone,
The demon reassumed his throne
In my faint heart . . . I dare not speak   35
My thoughts; but thus disturbed and weak
I sate and watched the vessels glide
Along the Ocean bright and wide,
Like spirit-wingèd chariots sent
O'er some serenest element   40
To ministrations strange and far;
As if to some Elysian star
They sailed for drink to medicine
Such sweet and bitter pain as mine. –
And the wind that winged their flight   45
From the land came fresh and light,
And the scent of sleeping flowers
And the coolness of the hours

Of dew, and the sweet warmth of day
Was scattered o'er the twinkling bay;   50
And the fisher with his lamp
And spear, about the low rocks damp
Crept, and struck the fish who came
To worship the delusive flame:
Too happy, they whose pleasure sought   55
Extinguishes all sense and thought
Of the regret that pleasure [,]
Seeking life alone, not peace.

from **The Triumph of Life**

Swift as a spirit hastening to his task
    Of glory and of good, the Sun sprang forth
Rejoicing in his splendour, and the mask

    Of darkness fell from the awakened Earth.
The smokeless altars of the mountain snows   5
    Flamed above crimson clouds, and at the birth

Of light, the Ocean's orison arose
    To which the birds tempered their matin lay.
All flowers in field or forest which unclose

    Their trembling eyelids to the kiss of day   10
Swinging their censers in the element,
    With orient incense lit by the new ray

Burned slow and inconsumably, and sent
    Their odorous sighs up to the smiling air,
And in succession due, did Continent,   15

    Isle, Ocean, and all things that in them wear
The form and character of mortal mould
    Rise as the Sun their father rose, to bear

Their portion of the toil which he of old
   Took as his own and then imposed on them;   20
But I, whom thoughts which must remain untold

   Had kept as wakeful as the stars that gem
The cone of night, now they were laid asleep,
   Stretched my faint limbs beneath the hoary stem

Which an old chestnut flung athwart the steep   25
   Of a green Apennine: before me fled
The night; behind me rose the day; the Deep

   Was at my feet, and Heaven above my head;
When a strange trance over my fancy grew
   Which was not slumber, for the shade it spread   30

Was so transparent that the scene came through
   As clear as when a veil of light is drawn
O'er evening hills, they glimmer; and I knew

   That I had felt the freshness of that dawn,
Bathed in the same cold dew my brow and hair,   35
   And sate as thus upon that slope of lawn

Under the self-same bough, and heard as there
   The birds, the fountains and the Ocean hold
Sweet talk in music through the enamoured air.

   And then a Vision on my brain was rolled . . .   40

As in that trance of wondrous thought I lay
   This was the tenor of my waking dream:
Methought I sate beside a public way

   Thick strewn with summer dust, and a great stream
Of people there was hurrying to and fro   45
   Numerous as gnats upon the evening gleam,

All hastening onward, yet none seemed to know
 Whither he went, or whence he came, or why
He made one of the multitude, yet so

Was borne amid the crowd as through the sky   50
One of the million leaves of summer's bier. –
 Old age and youth, manhood and infancy,

Mixed in one mighty torrent did appear,
 Some flying from the thing they feared and some
Seeking the object of another's fear,   55

And others as with steps towards the tomb
Pored on the trodden worms that crawled beneath,
 And others mournfully within the gloom

Of their own shadow walked, and called it death . . .
 And some fled from it as it were a ghost,   60
Half fainting in the affliction of vain breath.

But more, with motions which each other crossed,
Pursued or shunned the shadows the clouds threw
 Or birds within the noonday aether lost,

Upon that path where flowers never grew;   65
 And weary with vain toil and faint for thirst
Heard not the fountains whose melodious dew

Out of their mossy cells forever burst,
Nor felt the breeze which from the forest told
 Of grassy paths, and wood lawns interspersed   70

With overarching elms and caverns cold,
 And violet banks where sweet dreams brood, but they
Pursued their serious folly as of old . . .

And as I gazed methought that in the way
The throng grew wilder, as the woods of June   75
 When the south wind shakes the extinguished day –

And a cold glare, intenser than the noon
   But icy cold, obscured with light
The Sun as he the stars. Like the young moon

   When on the sunlit limits of the night   80
Her white shell trembles amid crimson air,
   And whilst the sleeping tempest gathers might

Doth, as a herald of its coming, bear
   The ghost of her dead mother, whose dim form
Bends in dark aether from her infant's chair,   85

   So came a chariot on the silent storm
Of its own rushing splendour, and a Shape
   So sate within as one whom years deform

Beneath a dusky hood and double cape
   Crouching within the shadow of a tomb,   90
And o'er what seemed the head, a cloud like crape

   Was bent, a dun and faint etherial gloom
Tempering the light; upon the chariot's beam
   A Janus-visaged Shadow did assume

The guidance of that wonder-wingèd team.   95
   The shapes which drew it in thick lightnings
Were lost: I heard alone on the air's soft stream

   The music of their ever-moving wings.
All the four faces of that charioteer
   Had their eyes banded . . . little profit brings   100

Speed in the van and blindness in the rear,
   Nor then avail the beams that quench the Sun,
Or that his banded eyes could pierce the sphere

   Of all that is, has been, or will be done. –
So ill was the car guided, but it passed   105
   With solemn speed majestically on . . .

The crowd gave way, and I arose aghast,
   Or seemed to rise, so mighty was the trance,
And saw like clouds upon the thunder-blast

   The million with fierce song and maniac dance   110
Raging around; such seemed the jubilee
   As when to greet some conqueror's advance

Imperial Rome poured forth her living sea
   From senate-house and prison and theatre,
When Freedom left those who upon the free   115

   Had bound a yoke which soon they stooped to bear.
Nor wanted here the true similitude
   Of a triumphal pageant, for where'er

The chariot rolled, a captive multitude
   Was driven; all those who had grown old in power   120
Or misery, – all who have their age subdued,

   By action or by suffering, and whose hour
Was drained to its last sand in weal or woe,
   So that the trunk survived both fruit and flower;

All those whose fame or infamy must grow   125
   Till the great winter lay the form and name
Of their green earth with them forever low,

   – All but the sacred few who could not tame
Their spirits to the Conqueror, but as soon
   As they had touched the world with living flame   130

Fled back like eagles to their native noon,
   Or those who put aside the diadem
Of earthly thrones or gems, till the last one

   Were there; – for they of Athens and Jerusalem
Were neither mid the mighty captives seen,   135
   Nor mid the ribald crowd that followed them

Or fled before . . . Now swift, fierce and obscene
   The wild dance maddens in the van, and those
Who lead it, fleet as shadows on the green,

   Outspeed the chariot and without repose   140
Mix with each other in tempestuous measure
   To savage music . . . Wilder as it grows,

They, tortured by the agonizing pleasure,
   Convulsed, and on the rapid whirlwinds spun
Of that fierce spirit, whose unholy leisure   145

   Was soothed by mischief since the world begun,
Throw back their heads and loose their streaming hair,
   And in their dance round her who dims the Sun

Maidens and youths fling their wild arms in air
   As their feet twinkle; they recede, and now   150
Bending within each other's atmosphere

   Kindle invisibly; and as they glow,
Like moths by light attracted and repelled,
   Oft to their bright destruction come and go,

Till – like two clouds into one vale impelled   155
   That shake the mountains when their lightnings mingle,
And die in rain, – the fiery band which held

   Their natures, snaps . . . ere the shock cease to tingle,
One falls and then another in the path
   Senseless, nor is the desolation single, –   160

Yet ere I can say *where*, the chariot hath
   Passed over them; nor other trace I find
But as of foam after the Ocean's wrath

   Is spent upon the desert shore. – Behind,
Old men, and women foully disarrayed   165
   Shake their grey hair in the insulting wind,

Limp in the dance and strain with limbs decayed
   To reach the car of light which leaves them still
Farther behind and deeper in the shade.

But not the less with impotence of will   170
They wheel, though ghastly shadows interpose
   Round them and round each other, and fulfil

Their part and to the dust whence they arose
   Sink, and corruption veils them as they lie,
And frost in these performs what fire in those.   175

Struck to the heart by this sad pageantry,
Half to myself I said, 'And what is this?
   Whose shape is that within the car? and why' –

I would have added – 'is all here amiss?'
   But a voice answered: 'Life' . . . I turned and knew   180
(O Heaven have mercy on such wretchedness!)

That what I thought was an old root which grew
To strange distortion out of the hill side
   Was indeed one of that deluded crew,

And that the grass which methought hung so wide   185
   And white, was but his thin discoloured hair,
And that the holes it vainly sought to hide

Were or had been eyes. – 'If thou canst forbear
To join the dance, which I had well forborne,'
   Said the grim Feature, of my thought aware,   190

'I will unfold that which to this deep scorn
   Led me and my companions, and relate
The progress of the pageant since the morn;

'If thirst of knowledge doth not thus abate,
Follow it even to the night, but I   195
   Am weary' . . . Then like one who with the weight

Of his own words is staggered wearily
   He paused, and ere he could resume, I cried,
'First who art thou?' . . . 'Before thy memory

  'I feared, loved, hated, suffered, did, and died,   200
And if the spark with which Heaven lit my spirit
   Earth had with purer nutriment supplied,

'Corruption would not now thus much inherit
   Of what was once Rousseau – nor this disguise
Stain that within which still disdains to wear it. –   205

   'If I have been extinguished, yet there rise
A thousand beacons from the spark I bore.'
   'And who are those chained to the car?' 'The wise,

'The great, the unforgotten: they who wore
   Mitres and helms and crowns, or wreaths of light,   210
Signs of thought's empire over thought; their lore

   'Taught them not this – to know themselves; their might
Could not repress the mutiny within,
   And for the morn of truth they feigned, deep night

'Caught them ere evening.' 'Who is he with chin   215
   Upon his breast, and hands crossed on his chain?'
'The child of a fierce hour; he sought to win

   'The world, and lost all it did contain
Of greatness, in its hope destroyed; and more
   Of fame and peace than Virtue's self can gain   220

'Without the opportunity which bore
   Him on its eagle's pinion to the peak
From which a thousand climbers have before

   'Fall'n as Napoleon fell.' – I felt my cheek
Alter to see the great form pass away   225
   Whose grasp had left the giant world so weak

That every pigmy kicked it as it lay –
   And much I grieved to think how power and will
In opposition rule our mortal day –

   And why God made irreconcilable   230
Good and the means of good; and for despair
   I half disdained mine eye's desire to fill

With the spent vision of the times that were
   And scarce have ceased to be . . . 'Dost thou behold,'
Said then my guide, 'those spoilers spoiled, Voltaire,   235

   'Frederick, and Kant, Catharine, and Leopold,
Each hoary anarch, demagogue and sage
   Whose name the fresh world thinks already old,

'For in the battle Life and they did wage
   She remained conqueror – I was overcome   240
By my own heart alone, which neither age

   'Nor tears nor infamy nor now the tomb
Could temper to its object.'

Notes

p. 3 Hymn to Intellectual Beauty Written late June 1816 (conceived during a voyage round Lake Geneva with Lord Byron). Published in the *Examiner* (19 Jan. 1817) and with *Rosalind and Helen* (1819). Shelley's hymn substitutes an abstract ideal for the received notion of divinity, and Love, Hope and Self-esteem for the orthodox virtues. 'Intellectual beauty' was a term whose resonances would have been familiar to many readers, including radicals, feminists and Romantic Hellenists.
27 name of God and ghosts and Heaven: Shelley's correction of the less blasphemously specific 'names of Demon, Ghost, and Heaven' (*Examiner*). **37 Self-esteem:** a proper valuation of one's own true worth (as opposed to self-contempt).

p. 5 Mont Blanc Written July 1816, dated 23 July by Shelley (the day of the expedition rather than of the completed poem, which had been transcribed by 29 Aug.). Published in *History of a Six Weeks' Tour* (1817).
1–11: Flowing through its ravine, the River Arve (which runs through Chamonix into Lake Geneva) supplies a metaphor for the relations between subject and object. **6 half its own:** because it renders and receives. **15 awful:** worthy of, or commanding, profound respect or reverential fear; solemnly impressive, sublimely majestic/causing dread. **27 unsculptured:** Shelley's journal entry of 21 July 1816 describes a waterfall which 'struck first on an enormous rock resembling precisely some colossal Egyptian statue of a female deity'. **strange sleep:** apparent immobility or silence in which 'thou [the ravine] dost lie'. **35ff:** the collaborative relationship between the external world and the perceiving mind. **separate fantasy:** cf. Shelley's account in a letter: 'All was as much our own as if we had been the creators of such impressions in the minds of others, as now occupied our own.' **43 that:** generally interpreted as the legion of wild thoughts. **thou:** the ravine. **47–8:** The sense is ambiguous, perhaps deliberately so. Either these images are derived from a Universe of Things outside the poet, perhaps from a Universal Mind – in which case the existence of the ravine in Shelley's mind depends on the permissive grace of a mysterious force; or they are maintained in existence by Shelley's

own mind. **53 unfurled:** spread out (thus cutting off Shelley's vision) or drawn aside. **71–4:** references to widely held theories on the volcanic origin of mountains. **79:** 'But for such faith' is puzzling and may be the result of a mistake in copying; it has been suggested that Shelley intended 'But' as an adverb meaning 'only'. 'But for' appears in the draft, although it originally read 'In such a faith', as does the intermediate fair copy in Shelley's hand. **86 daedal:** artful, carefully wrought. **96ff:** The natural scene can teach the attentive observer that no divinity is present in this creation; if it does exist, it dwells apart, as unconcerned as the mountain peak. **105 distinct:** marked in a manner so as to be distinguished; decorated, adorned.

p. 9 Ozymandias Written late 1817. Published in the *Examiner* (11 Jan. 1818) under the name *Glirastes* (dormouse [Shelley's family nickname] or dormouse as preacher). Ozymandias is the Greek name for the Pharaoh Ramses II, who reigned from 1279 to 1213 BC.
1 a traveller: conceivably Walter Coulson, editor of *The Traveller*, who visited the Shelleys in late 1817, or a reference to Robert Pococke's *A Description of the East* (1743), which portrays several statues of Ramses and of Memnon in various stages of disintegration. The poem is deliberately unspecific and flexible in its use of facts. **6–8:** The passions depicted in the statue survive both the sculptor's hand and the heart of the pharaoh who gave them life. **mocked:** imitated (perhaps with a hint of silent irony).

p. 10 Stanzas Written in Dejection, near Naples Written Dec. 1818. Published posthumously (1824). In a letter of the same month Shelley recorded that he had 'depression enough of spirits & not good health'; the main causes were the death of his daughter in September and the subsequent estrangement from Mary – but dejection was a recurrent condition with the Romantic poets.
22 The sage: possibly Socrates or Diogenes.

p. 11 Julian and Maddalo Begun probably in Sept. 1818 and finished by 15 Aug. 1819, when it was sent to Leigh Hunt for anonymous publication. Published posthumously (1824). The poem had its origins in a meeting and conversation between Shelley and Byron at Venice on 23 Aug. 1818. Julian is based on Shelley, Maddalo on Byron, and Maddalo's child on Allegra, Byron's daughter by Claire Clairmont, who had been sent to Venice in April, and concern for whose future was the reason for Shelley's visit. The name 'Maddalo' (accented on the first syllable) was derived from a courtier in Tasso's circle while 'Julian' was the central figure in an unfinished poem by Byron. The madman 'is also in some degree a painting from nature, but, with respect to time and place, ideal'. It has been suggested that he was based on Torquato Tasso (1544–95), author of *Gerusalemme liberata*, whose predicament inspired Shelley to begin a fragmentary play (Goethe's *Torquato Tasso* had appeared in 1790, and Byron's *Lament of Tasso* in July 1817).

87 station: a point at which one stands to obtain a view. **117:** Shelley could not swim, as Byron would have known since they were together in a boat during a storm on Lake Geneva in 1816. **173:** The punctuation is intended (similar constructions are common in Shelley). The sense is: 'We might be as happy, high, majestical as in our wildest dreams'. **188 those . . . philosophy:** the Greek philosophers, who dispassionately analysed the great problems of existence before the Christian Church inhibited philosophical and theological speculation. **204:** Cf. 'there is some soul of goodness in things evil,/Would men observingly distil it out' (*Henry V*, IV.i.3–4). **214:** San Servolo (or San Servilio) is an island with a Benedictine monastery which in 1725 became an asylum for 'maniacs of noble family or comfortable circumstances' under the care of the Hospital Fathers of St John of God. A hospital and church (still standing) were built between 1734 and 1759. In 1797, under Napoleonic influence, class distinctions were abolished. **238 peculiar:** personal, relating exclusively to himself. **244 humourist:** a man subject to humours; fantastical, whimsical. **517 in his society:** in company with him. **536 nice:** refined. **gentleness:** although the Maniac *is* an inoffensive creature, gentleness here specifically implies the behaviour of a gentleman. **587 Armenia:** Byron had been studying Armenian in 1817–18.

p. 24 Prometheus Unbound Written autumn 1818 (Act I), spring 1819 (Acts II and III), autumn 1819 (Act IV). Published 1820. Shelley's lyrical drama takes as its starting point the *Prometheus Bound* of Aeschylus but, in spite of incidental debts, is a highly original and independent work which explores and celebrates man's capacity to liberate himself from tyranny, both external and internal. Act IV (from which this extract is taken) marks the regeneration of humanity with a cosmic celebration. This visionary passage draws on Shelley's scientific reading in its poetic presentation of infra-red emanations and of the dance of matter, and on James Parkinson's *Organic Remains of a Former World* (1804–11) in its geology.

5 Æolian modulations: like the music of the Aeolian harp, which was played by the wind. **24 Mother of the Months:** the moon. **26 interlunar:** belonging to the period between the old and the new moons. **30 Regard:** look. **47 fire that is not brightness:** a reference perhaps to the ideas of Herschel and Davy on infra-red rays. **63 intertranspicuous:** that can be seen through or between each other (a word apparently invented by Shelley). **65 sightless:** invisible (as well, perhaps, as blind). **89 tyrant-quelling myrtle:** the swords with which Harmodius and Aristogeiton assassinated the Athenian tyrant Hipparchus were famously covered with myrtle, which was associated with love. **97 adamant:** rock or mineral renowned for its hardness. **98 Valueless:** beyond valuation. **104 ermine:** the white fur of ermine is usually associated with Kings, judges and peers. **108 targes:** shields. **117 fanes:** temples. **120 anatomies:** skeletons. **127 behemoth:** an enormous creature (see Job 40:15).

p. 27 The Mask of Anarchy Written Sept. 1819 and sent for publication in the *Examiner* on the 23rd. Published posthumously (1832). On 16 Aug. 1819 Henry Hunt was addressing a crowd of 60,000 working people in Manchester on the subject of parliamentary reform, when the militia attempted to arrest him. In the ensuing confusion, they were joined by a detachment of regular cavalry, who charged the crowd: the toll was fifteen dead and 500 injured (both approximate figures). Because it took place on St Peter's Fields this unhappy incident became known as 'Peterloo' (with ironical reference to Wellington's success on another field). The 'Mask' of the title refers to the allegorical pageant, the masquerade which gives the poem its basic shape; it also suggests the impostures and deceits of authority. 'Anarchy' implies that despotic power is allied to chaos and disorder rather than to true authority.

1–4: Shelley is following the conventions of visionary poetry. **6 Castlereagh:** Robert Stewart, Viscount Castlereagh (1769–1822), Foreign Secretrary since 1812. **8 Seven bloodhounds:** the seven states (Austria, Bourbon France, Portugal, Prussia, Russia, Spain, Sweden) which, with England, agreed in 1815 to postpone indefinitely the abolition of the slave trade. **15:** the Lord Chancellor in his robes (ermine was a symbol f purity). Eldon was famous for weeping in public. **24 Sidmouth:** Home Secretary, who raised large sums of money to build churches for the industrial poor, whom he repressed through the activities of the police and a complex network of spies, informers and *agents provocateurs*. **30–3:** 'And I looked, and behold a pale horse; and his name that sat on him was Death, and Hell followed with him' (Revelation 6:8). **82–3:** In 1817

Habeas Corpus had been suspended on suspicion of a plot to seize the Bank of England and the Tower of London. Here, that seizure of the focal points of power is carried out by government itself. **110 a Shape:** This has been identified both as Liberty and as Public Enlightenment (Leigh Hunt), but Shelley deliberately avoids specificity. **145 accent:** speech, utterance. **148 unwritten:** a story which is yet to be written and whose potential is therefore unfulfilled; perhaps, also, with an implication that the poor and the underprivileged had previously been excluded from the annals of history (unlike the 'storied dead' of Thomas Gray's 'Elegy'). **176ff. the Ghost of Gold:** paper money. **180ff:** A paper currency might eventually force the people to lose control of their own will and to indulge the desire to fight back — two serious infringements of Shelley's ethical ideals. **197–208:** 'The foxes have holes, and the birds of the air have nests; but the Son of man hath nowhere to lay his head' (Matthew 8:20). **220 Fame:** rumour. **245:** Britain, Austria, Prussia, Holland, Spain and Sardinia formed a coalition against revolutionary France in 1793. **250–1:** perhaps like Mary Magdalen, as a sign of repentance and submission (Luke 7:45). **like him following Christ:** Zacchaeus (Luke 19:1–10). **305 targes:** shields. **319–20 scimitars:** short, curved, single-edged swords, used among Orientals, especially Turks and Persians. **sphereless stars:** stars shooting from their spheres, i.e. meteors **330 phalanx:** a compact body of people massed or ranged in order or, more generally, a group banded together for a common purpose. **366 oracular:** traditionally, oracular responses were thought to be inspired by the inhalation of volcanic vapours.

p. 39 Ode to the West Wind Written late Oct. 1819. Published with *Prometheus Unbound* (1820).
4 hectic: feverish. **9 azure sister:** the gentle west wind of spring, usually masculine (Zephyrus or Favonius). **15–18:** fractocumulus or scud, 'clouds running beside thunderstorms, which can be seen discharging water into the sea but which themselves are composed of water evaporated from the sea' (Ludlam): these 'opposing streams of liquid and of vapour' suggest the 'tangled boughs'. **20–3 locks:** not to be confused with the loose clouds, these are 'the equally high but dense plume of fibrous cloud which reaches far ahead of the towering cloud columns at the heart of a thunderstorm' (Ludlam). **34 intenser day:** of a deeper blue than the sky. **42 despoil:** strip (of their leaves). **51 striven:** perhaps as Jacob wrestled with the angel. **63 dead thoughts:** his unsuccessful poems.

p. 42 Peter Bell the Third Written late Oct. 1819 and sent to Leigh

Hunt on 2 Nov. for publication. Published posthumously (1839). Shelley was inspired by two reviews in the *Examiner:* Keats's review of *Peter Bell: A Lyrical Ballad* by John Hamilton Reynolds (a spoof and parody of Wordsworth's *Peter Bell*, whose appearance it antedated by a week), and Hunt's review of Wordsworth's poem. *Peter Bell the Third* was so named because it was now the third poem in a sequence.

6–7: John Castle, informer and *agent provocateur*, George Canning, liberal Tory; William Cobbett, journalist, pamphleteer and influential radical; Viscount Castlereagh, Foreign Secretary. **9 cozening:** cheating, defrauding by deceit. **trepanning:** catching in a trap, luring into a course of action, swindling. **11:** The name of Southey is cancelled in the fair copy. **16 Chancery Court:** the court presided over by the Lord Chancellor where in 1817 Shelley was deprived of the custody of his two children by Harriet. **30 methodism:** Gin, suicide and Methodism all offer strategies of despair. **37 *amant miserè:*** love miserably (that is, give voice to their love by caterwauling). **41 hobnobbers:** those who drink together, or to each other, or are on familiar terms. **44 stockjobbers:** members of the Stock Exchange who deal in stocks on their own account. **56 levees:** assemblies held by a prince or person of distinction. **63 a Cretan-tonguèd panic:** a panic based on unreliable rumours; apprehension in relation to financial and commercial matters. **66–7 conversazioni:** social gatherings for the discussion of the arts or for learned conversation. **conventicles:** meetings or assemblies of a clandestine, irregular or illegal character; meetings of Nonconformists or Dissenters from the Church of England for religious worship. **76–85:** Damnation is not a sentence passed by a divine judge but a condition resulting from a free and deliberate choice. Hell is not a place so much as a state of mind which man imposes on himself. **flams:** humbug, deception. **92–3:** Shelley was frightened that Cobbett's demagoguery would incite the poor and the oppressed to violent revolution which would not lead them to the kingdom of Heaven promised to them in the Sermon on the Mount (Matthew 5). **96–100:** an ironical picture of Shelley the idealist. **117 Peter . . . square:** Wordsworth moving in polite society. **147–56:** Shelley suggests a certain narrowness of perspective, an egotistical limitation in Wordsworth. **167ff:** cf. 'Turned to a formal puritan,/ A solemn and unsexual man (550–1 in complete text of *Peter Bell the Third*). **173 a sister's kiss:** This may be an ironical allusion to Wordsworth's relations with Dorothy. **174 Diogenes:** a cynic philosopher, famous for his contempt of the flesh and of bodily comforts. **182–4:** 'Mouth for kisses was never the worse: rather, it renews as the moon does' (moral of Boccaccio, *Decameron, 217*).

p. 49 England in 1819 Written late 1819 and sent to Leigh Hunt for publication. Published posthumously (1839).
1: a combination perhaps of King Lear and Gloucester. *King Lear* was too politically sensitive to be staged during the Regency period. George III was soon to die (29 Jan. 1820) at the age of 81, sixty years after coming to the throne. He had been irremediably insane since 1811. **2 Princes:** the sons of George III, notorious for their coarse tastes, dissolute habits and ostentatious extravagance. **7:** See notes to *The Mask of Anarchy*: St Peter's Fields, where the demonstrators were stabbed by the militia might have been cultivated to save them from starvation. **10:** a legal system based on violence ('sanguine': bloody) and on mercenary considerations ('Golden'); 'tempt and slay' refers to the government's use of *agents provocateurs* who stimulated revolution in order that it might be put down *pour encourager les autres.* **12:** the unreformed Parliament.

p. 50 The Cloud Written probably early 1820. Published with *Prometheus Unbound* (1820).
17–30: According to Adam Walker, 'water rises through the air, flying on the wings of electricity'. The 'pilot' is the electricity which guides the cloud; there is a mutual attraction between this positive force and the negative electricity below ('the genii', 'The Spirit he loves'), which results in thunderstorms or rain. The informing principle of the cloud remains intact even though the cloud itself may disappear. **dissolving:** can be read as both transitive and intransitive. **58 these:** the stars. **71 sphere-fire-** **:** the sun. **75 pores:** Erasmus Darwin referred to 'each nice pore of ocean, earth, and air', while Adam Walker described how rain 'sinks into the chinks and pores of the ground'. The cloud is mainly formed by 'sweat' drawn up by the sun from the sea, rivers and rivulets. **79 convex:** 'The earth's atmosphere bends a ray of sunlight into a curve . . . convex to an observer in a cloud looking down' (King-Hele). The difference from the limited perspective of troubled humanity is tactfully suggested. **81–4:** The empty tomb ('cenotaph') is unbuilt as the cloud fills the sky and the blue dome disappears.

p. 52 Men of England: A Song Written 1819. Published posthumously (1839). On 1 May 1820 Shelley asked Leigh Hunt if he 'knew of any bookseller who would like to publish a little volume of *popular songs* wholly political, & destined to awaken & direct the imagination of the reformers'. This book was never completed, but Shelley did write a number of poems which seemed to meet his own criteria.

9: The central image of bees and drones draws upon a commonplace in contemporary radical discourse which identified the working classes with bees. **27–8:** Shelley envisages another Peterloo or perhaps the frustration of those strategies for peaceful reform which are set out in *The Mask of Anarchy*. **27:** The manuscript appears to read 'when see'; Mary Shelley's version reads 'Ye see'.

p. 53 To a Sky-lark Written summer 1820 (probably June). Published with *Prometheus Unbound* (1820).
5 unpremeditated: unplanned. **8 a cloud of fire:** Primarily, this means a cloud illuminated by the setting sun but it may also refer to the *nuée ardente* of a volcano. **22 silver sphere:** Venus (the morning star) which gradually disappears with the coming of daylight. **37 In the light of thought:** The poet's personal identity is subsumed in the radiance of inspiration. **66 Hymenaeal:** for a wedding. **86:** Cf. *Hamlet*, IV.iv.37.

p. 56 Letter to Maria Gisborne Written late June 1820, posted 1 July. Published posthumously (1824). The original letter is not extant. This verse ⋯ private letter and which Shelley ⋯ as written when the Shelleys were ⋯ friends John and Maria Gisborne, ⋯ been a friend of the Godwins and ⋯ nish. The workshop described in ⋯ son, Henry Reveley, a nautical ⋯ ning a steamboat with Shelley's

⋯les, Sicilian mathematician and ⋯e 'On Bodies Floating in Fluids'. ⋯or device; machine; product of ⋯athematical calculations, which ⋯hrase combines the geometrical ⋯ctivate magic spells with the ⋯ **10 Vulcan:** blacksmith and ⋯ a wheel in Hades for seducing ⋯ven and Earth who rebelled ⋯with the giants whose later ⋯t **Dominic:** founder of the ⋯ Inquisition. **13ff:** Philip II's ⋯f 1588; their Catholic faith ⋯tants were doomed to eternal damnation because they were outside the fold of the Church. **19–20:** '. . . Ferdinand has proclaimed the Constitution of 1812 & called the Cortes – The Inquisition is abolished. The dungeons opened & the Patriots pouring out' (Mary Shelley to Maria Gisborne, 31 Mar. 1820). **31 Proteus:** the old man of the sea, who could assume any shape in order to elude capture. **37 Tubal Cain:** according to Genesis (4:23) the first artificer in brass and iron. **41 knacks:** ingenious contrivances, toys, quips; odd and whimsical trifles. **45 swink:** labour, toil. **51 rouse:** a full draught of liquor, a bumper. **61:** a rough model in the form of a paper boat. **81:** a famous mathematician and astronomer; the authors of textbooks on geometry and algebra. **84 Baron de Tott:** author of the popular *Mémoires sur les Turcs et les Tartares* (1784). **89–90 many mo:** Spenser, *Faerie Queene*, IV.i.8 (*mo* = more). **'womb of time':** *Othello*, I.iii.377. **92 Archimage:** the great enchanter in Spenser's *Faerie Queene*. **95–8:** On 26 June, Shelley remonstrated with Robert Southey on the offensively personal and un-Christian spirit of the review of *The Revolt of Islam* in the *Quarterly* for Apr. 1819. **100 Libeccio:** the south-west wind.

p. 60 The Witch of Atlas Written 14–16 Aug. 1820. Sent to Charles Ollier for publication on 20 Jan. 1821. Published posthumously (1824). This 'visionary rhyme' was written in *ottava rima*, the main verse form of Italian narrative poetry, which had been successfully appropriated for English by Byron and which Shelley had recently employed in his translation of the Homeric *Hymn to Mercury*. The Witch is Shelley's own invention, an inscrutable, subversive and playful figure, partly modelled on the divinities of Greek mythology, deliberately beyond the simplicities of easy interpretation. **7 fanes:** temples. **50 diaphanous:** so light and insubstantial as to be almost transparent. **65–71:** Aurora (or Eos) was in love with Tithonus who was granted immortality but not eternal youth; Proserpina (Persephone) allowed Adonis to return from the underworld to his lover Venus (Aphrodite) for six months in each year. **72 Heliad:** the Witch of Atlas (as daughter of the sun). **75–6:** Diana, goddess of the moon, was in love with the mortal Endymion (the subject of a long poem by Keats published in 1818). **82 panacea:** remedy for all diseases. **114 hieroglyphics:** the ancient Egyptian mode of writing which used pictures or objects representing words or syllables (with an implication of difficulty or of the secrecy involved in a sacred code). **120 pastoral letters:** letters from a bishop to his flock in the region of his jurisdiction (diocese). **130 somnambulism:** sleep-walking. **131–3:** The one-eyed Cyclopses forged thunderbolts for

Zeus (Jupiter) in the smithy of Vulcan (Hephaestus), the god of fire and metalworking, who was associated with volcanoes (**abysm** = bowels of the earth). Turning swords to ploughshares traditionally signified peace in biblical and classical literature. **136: Amasis** king of Egypt, lived 570–526 B.C.

p. 64 To the Moon Written 1820 or 1821. Published posthumously (1824). After a gap, the manuscript continues: 'Thou chosen sister of the spirit / That gazes on thee till it pities.' Shelley may have intended to relate this symbol of alienation to a specific human or dramatic context.

p. 65 Epipsychidion Written after Dec. 1820; finished 16 Feb. 1821. Published anonymously (1821). The title has been interpreted as 'soul out of my soul', 'soul within the soul' and 'a little additional soul' but might be read as 'little soul song'. The poem charts a personal history of love, false and true, making use of an idealized framework largely derived from Dante. **1 She:** Teresa Emilia Viviani, with whom Shelley had a brief, idealized relationship and to whom this poem is addressed, was the daughter of the governor of Pisa, who had been confined to a convent to await the selection of a suitable husband. **14–15 stops Of planetary music:** cadences of the music of the spheres, audible ('heard in trance') to those who rise above the restrictions of everyday consciousness. **20ff:** This passage combines the language of science with that of religious devotion. Diffusion is 'the spontaneous molecular mixing or inter-penetration of two fluids without chemical combination', hence the inter-mixture is 'unentangled'. **Stains:** colours. **unintermitted:** continuous. **29:** Shelley's draft is very confused but it appears that he may have intended a plural and omitted to make the necessary changes. **46 third sphere:** the sphere of Venus or love (*il terzo ciel*). **50–1:** April is made flesh, Frost is a skeleton. **89ff True Love:** ideal love) was originally 'Free Love' but Shelley abandoned this because its connotations are misleading.

p. 68 Adonais Written between mid-April and early June 1821. Published July 1821. The poem mourns the recent death of Keats, whom Shelley did not know well but whom he had invited to recuperate in his house at Pisa. Shelley assumes that Keats's demise had been accelerated by the harsh treatment received by *Endymion* in the *Quarterly Review* for Apr. 1818. The title is probably derived from Bion's *Lament for Adonis*, a Hellenistic elegy part of which he translated, conflated with *Adonai*, the Hebrew word for 'Lord'.

5 thy obscure compeers: hours which have not been selected for such prominent duties. **11–12 shaft . . . darkness:** the anonymous review in the *Quarterly*. **12 Urania:** the Muse of poetry and therefore the mother of Adonais/Keats. **14 Paradise:** park or pleasure-garden; also heaven, since Urania is a heavenly muse. **29–36:** the disillusionment of 'republican' Milton, who died only eight years after the Restoration. **third among the sons of light:** the third great epic poet in succession to Homer and Dante. **39–43:** Successful minor poets have known more happiness than greater spirits whose potential was thwarted or never realized. **51 extreme:** last, latest. **55 that high Capital:** Rome. **63 liquid:** pure, free from harshness or discord. **69 The eternal Hunger:** decomposition. **94 anadem:** headband, chaplet, garland. **99 the barbèd fire:** the fire of love's arrows. **107 clips:** embraces. **120–3:** The clouds of early morning obscured the last stars instead of falling as dew. In many societies, particularly in the East, unbound hair is a sign of mourning. **127:** Echo has abandoned her usual functions. **133–4:** Narcissus rejected the advances of Echo, who pined away till she was only a voice. **141–4:** Hyacinth was loved by Phoebus Apollo, who killed him by accident. Narcissus fell in love with his own reflection. After death both became flowers, who now exhale signs of compassion ('ruth') rather than sweet scents. **145–51 spirit's sister:** Keats had written 'Ode to a Nightingale'. **147–8 scale Heaven:** in epic poems like that about the sun-god Hyperion. **159–60 brake:** thicket. **brere:** bush or shrub. **174–6:** The flowers illuminate death by their fragrance, as the stars illumine night by their splendour (light). **177–9 that . . . knows:** the mind of man. **sightless:** invisible. **185–9:** Since death is our creditor, the condition on which we enjoy the beauties of nature is the inevitability of time, change, sorrow. **195 their sister:** the Echo who had recited Adonais's poems. **202 ghost:** soul, principle of life. **204–6 So:** in this way. **219 Blushed to annihilation:** since a blush brings blood to the face it negates the pallor of death. **228 heartless:** disheartened, dejected. **234 I am chained to Time:** because she is the Muse of mortal poets. **240 the mirrored shield:** like that used by Perseus to kill the Gorgon Medusa – by reflecting the image of her head, the sight of which turned observers to stone. **242 crescent:** increasing. **249–52:** Byron smote and silenced his critics with *English Bards and Scotch Reviewers* (1809) as Apollo killed the dragon Python. **262 mountain shepherds:** The pastoral mode is used to introduce a procession of contemporary poets. **264 Pilgrim of Eternity:** Byron, author of *Childe Harold's Pilgrimage*. **268–70:** Thomas Moore, gave voice to the sad condition of Ireland

('Ierne') in his *Irish Melodies*. **271 one frail Form:** Shelley himself in mythological guise. **276 Actaeon-like:** Actaeon saw Artemis (Diana) naked, for which he was changed into a stag and then devoured by his own dogs. **280 pardlike:** like the leopard, which was sacred to Dionysus. **283 superincumbent:** which lies or presses on him. **291–2:** The *thyrsus* was a staff traditionally carried by Dionysus and his Bacchantes (cypress for mourning here replacing the original pine-cone). In Plato's *Ion*, which Shelley translated, poets are compared to the Bacchantes. **298 partial:** prejudiced, for reasons explained in 300. **307–15:** Leigh Hunt was one of the first to recognize the promise of Keats. **316 drunk poison:** in the course of the poem the death of Adonais is accounted for in a variety of ways. **319 nameless worm:** the anonymous reviewer in the *Quarterly*. **327 noteless:** of no note, undistinguished. **338:** a reference to the Burial of the Dead. **381–5 plastic stress:** shaping, moulding, creative principle. **395–6:** The great minds of the past are a vital influence. **397–405:** a list of poets who were cut off before maturity, like Keats, Thomas Chatterton, Sir Philip Sidney and the Roman poet Lucan (who died respectively aged 17, 32 and 26). **414 Vesper:** Hesperus, the evening star (mentioned in Epigraph, not printed here). **415–23:** Learn to acknowledge the vastness of the universe and the minuteness of the individual and moderate your misgivings and fear of death. **417: pendulous:** suspended (in space). **439–50:** Shelley's young son William was buried in the Protestant Cemetery which lies next to the pyramidal tomb of Caius Cestius. **463 Stains:** enriches by colouring (as in stained glass); but see 356. **477:** perhaps a reference to the marriage service. **484 are mirrors:** more correctly 'is a mirror', but Shelley is thinking of the multiplicity of the web of being.

p. 83 The Aziola Written 1821 (probably at the Baths of San Giuliano, near Pisa, between May and the end of Oct.). Published posthumously (1829). Mary remembered: 'the cicale at noon-day kept up their hum; the aziola cooed in the quiet evening.' The aziola is a small owl (*assiolo*).

p. 84 Hellas Written autumn 1821. Published 1822. *Hellas* (Greece) celebrates the Greek rising against the Turks but ends on a note of uncertainty in this chorus of Greek captive women. Shelley comments: 'The final chorus is indistinct and obscure, as the event of the living drama whose arrival it foretells'. In particular, he was afraid that the Holy Alliance would help the Turks to crush the rising.

4 weeds: garments usually associated with mourning. **12 Cyclads:** a group of islands in the Aegean Sea. **13 Argo:** ship in which Jason recovered the Gold Fleece ('prize'). **17–18:** Ulysses was seduced by Calypso on his way home from the Trojan War. **21–4:** By solving the Sphinx's riddle, Oedipus liberated Thebes from the plague; but he also murdered his father Laius, with tragic consequences. **31–4 Saturn and Love:** 'among the deities of a real or imaginary state of innocence and happiness' ('The Golden Years'). **all who fell:** the gods of Greece, Asia, and Egypt, superseded by Christ ('One who rose'). **many unsubdued:** 'the monstrous objects of the idolatry of China, India, the Antarctic islands, and the native tribes of America' (Shelley's note). **39–40:** Cf. 'Yet shall some few traces of olden sin lurk behind . . . a second warfare, too, shall there be, and again shall a great Achilles be sent to Troy' (Virgil, *Fourth Eclogue*).

p. 85 O World, O Life, O Time Dated 1821 by Mary Shelley. Published posthumously (1824).
8: Shelley left a gap for an adjective to describe summer.

p. 86 One Word Is Too Often Profaned Dated 1821 by Mary Shelley. Published posthumously (1824).

p. 86 To Jane (The keen stars were twinkling) Written June 1822. Published posthumously (1832; 1839). Jane Williams and her husband Edward had arrived in Pisa in Jan. 1821. They shared a house with the Shelleys at San Terenzo in the summer of 1822. Shelley admired Jane's musical gifts and presented her with a guitar (see 'With a Guitar to Jane'). **17 dews:** in the sense of the adjective 'liquid' (pure and clear in tone).

p. 87 Lines Written in the Bay of Lerici Written late June 1822. Published posthumously (1862). These roughly drafted and untitled lines refer to Shelley's friendship with Jane Williams.
10–12: Albatrosses are reputed to sleep on the wing. **21–4:** Jane has hypnotic powers. **39–44:** The ships are associated with daemons, spirits intermediary between man and God who are the good angels of Shelley's universe. **55–8:** The poet reflects on a concentration of purpose which is single-mindedly committed to the pursuit of pleasure and oblivious to its final consequences. **58:** Shelley's textual intentions here are not clear nor is it certain whether the poem was meant to conclude with this generalized reflection.

p. 89 The Triumph of Life Probably written between late May and the end of June 1822. Published posthumously from very rough drafts in 1824. This was Shelley's last major poem and was left unfinished and unrevised at his death. The Life of the title is life seen as conqueror and destroyer of man and his ideals, a grim and relentless process which only a heroic few can honourably resist.

5 smokeless altars: as opposed to the altars of human religion with their offerings of sacrifice. **7 orison:** prayer. **23 cone of night:** earth's shadow in space. **29 strange trance:** the prelude to a visionary poem. **87 its:** the sleeping tempest's. **91 cloud like crape:** originally 'a widow's veil of crape'. **94 Janus-visaged:** with faces at back and front. **103 banded:** blindfolded. **111–16:** a typical triumph under the Roman Empire. **121 their age:** probably their period in history. **126 the great winter:** the end of the world. **132 diadem:** crown. **134 they . . . Jerusalem:** Socrates and Jesus, in Shelley's view the greatest figures in human history. **137ff:** the dance of sexual attraction ('that fierce spirit'). **175:** Impotence destroys the old ('these'), sensuality the young ('those'). **204 Rousseau:** Jean-Jacques Rousseau (1712–78), whose political writings and romantic novel *La Nouvelle Héloïse* Shelley greatly admired but whose *Confessions* 'gave license to passions that only incapacitate and contract the human heart', **210: wreaths of light:** a combination of the laurel wreath of the poet and the halo, here a sign of intellectual rather than spiritual achievement. **211–15:** They failed to acquire self-knowledge and so were unable to achieve the necessary internal equilibrium. **226–7:** presumably a reference to the outcome of the Napoleonic wars and the establishment of the Holy Alliance. **235–6:** two sages, Voltaire (i.e. François-Marie Arouet [1694–1778]), whose incisive and capacious critical intelligence epitomized the Enlightenment, and Immanuel Kant (1724–1804), author of *The Critique of Judgement* (1790); and three benevolent rulers (Frederick the Great of Prussia, Catherine the Great of Russia, Leopold II of Austria). **237 anarchs:** see headnote to *The Mask of Anarchy*. **240–3:** Unlike the others who were conquered by the temptations of the external world, Rousseau was led astray by his own better qualities. **243 temper:** Elsewhere in *The Triumph of Life* this word has positive connotations which Rousseau here seems to override.